First Impressions

The British Discovery of Australia

Margaret Steven

British Museum (Natural History)

Through this book and the accompanying exhibition unfolds a remarkable story of discovery and settlement in Australia.

In the difficult early years of the colony artists and scientists created a breathtaking record of events. Today, the collections held by the British Museum (Natural History) are an unparalleled and beautiful legacy of their work.

These unique records have survived to be seen in the year celebrating the bicentenary of European settlement of Australia. Their presence here is a fitting tribute to the spirit of human endeavour that was to transform a miserable penal colony into a great independent nation.

H.R.H. The Duke of Kent
President
The Britain-Australia Bicentennial
   Committee

Contents

Foreword

In 1979, the Australian Government announced its intention of establishing The Australian Bicentennial Authority to plan and co-ordinate a national programme of celebrations in 1988 to commemorate the bicentenary of the first European settlement in Australia. The themes for the celebrations are 'Living Together' and 'Celebration of a Nation'.

In 1984, I was asked by the British Government to plan and co-ordinate the United Kingdom's participation in the celebrations. The Britain-Australia Bicentennial Committee was formed in London with National and Regional Committees in the United Kingdom, as well as Special Sub-Committees for Agriculture, Arts, Education, Exhibitions, Maritime, Publications, Social, Sport, Science, Technology, Industry and Medicine; Souvenirs and Tourism. An Endorsement Scheme was established to give special recognition to the large number of projects, activities and events planned for 1987 and 1988.

Following the recommendation by The Britain-Australia Bicentennial Committee that the United Kingdom's official 'Bicentennial Gift' should be a sail training ship, *Young Endeavour* was named on 2nd June 1987 by Her Royal Highness The Duchess of Kent and sailed from Cowes for Australia on 3rd August.

First Impressions – the British Discovery of Australia is one of the most important events in the British celebrations which include sporting events, conferences, Australia Week in cities and towns in the United Kingdom, the establishment of a Schools Linking Scheme and an Educational Trust, and tours of Australia by representative British cultural and performing arts groups, as well as reciprocal tours by Australian groups to Britain. It is therefore all the more fitting that *First Impressions* after being shown in London is making one of the most extensive tours ever by an international exhibition in Australia.

I hope the programme of events will help to make 1988 a memorable year for all and will strengthen the close ties which exist between our two great countries.

Sir Peter Gadsden GBE
Chairman,
The Britain-Australia Bicentennial Committee

Introduction

Before Magellan proved the world was round in 1522, sailing beyond the horizon took great courage. Gradually, superstitions about the oceans faded, to be replaced by a period of great European exploration. With cross staffs, astrolobes and compasses the Spanish and Portuguese steered their small ships south, showing the way over the next 200 years to the Dutch, British and French.

Drawn by the riches of the East Indies, it was inevitable that these traders would soon find Australia. But the Dutch quickly lost interest in this new land – successive landfalls on the northern and western coasts showed it to be a barren, inhospitable place. The last significant Dutch voyage in 1642 was led by Abel Tasman. He circumnavigated the Australian mainland, defining its outer limits and putting Tasmania on the map. It was then left to the British to discover the fertile eastern coast, and make it their prize.

The presence of a giant southern continent was a popular theory in the mid 1800s. The Royal Society's voyage to record the transit of Venus in Tahiti also included secret orders for Captain Cook to go on in search of this mysterious Pacific land. The voyage of the *Endeavour* was to alter dramatically British interest in Australia. At the time, Britain was facing social, industrial and scientific revolutions, and when the treasures from the *Endeavour* expedition to New South Wales arrived back in Britain they fired the imagination of the scientific community.

Led by Joseph Banks, scientists and artists had collected and recorded a wealth of new Australian specimens. These finds were astounding, and threatened to upset scientific thought of the time. The great success of the voyage paved the way for many more scientific explorations to the Pacific, carrying both scientists and artists as recorders.

Joseph Banks subsequently became President of the Royal Society, and used his position to push for the choice of Botany Bay as a British penal colony. After the war with France and loss of the American colony, this new continent with untapped resources seemed a highly attractive option.

In 1788, the First Convict Fleet reached New South Wales. Supplies never arrived, crops failed and starvation set in, but against all these odds the settlement slowly took shape. At a time when patronage was a way of life, the success of the early settlement and the Royal Societies' interests in natural science were irrevocably linked. All the communications sent back to Britain – reports of expeditions and encounters with native Australians – carried with them a profusion of specimens, written descriptions and drawings of the land and its wildlife.

Further expeditions took botanists such as George Caley and Alan Cunningham to this unexplored land. These scientific forays reached a peak in 1802 when Matthew Flinders circumnavigated the continent in the *Investigator*. Not only did this result in the first complete outline of Australia but it also led to some of the most scientifically accurate and beautiful paintings of Australian plants and animals. These were the work of the artist Ferdinand Bauer and the botanist Robert Brown.

The colony remained a place of scientific curiosity right into the 1800s, and this attitude only began to disappear with Banks's death in 1820. Gradually the colony developed its own way of life, with its own industries, until at last internal matters took priority.

A Message from the Director

My colleagues and I at the British Museum (Natural History) appreciated the challenge to celebrate the Australian Bicentenary with a stunning exhibition and this entertaining and delightfully presented volume.

***First Impressions** has provided the opportunity to display to everyone some of the historic and very beautiful prints and drawings from the Museum's collections in an exhibition which brings together art, history and science. We hope visitors to **First Impressions** will be excited and enthralled by its displays. Should you have been unable to see the exhibition then this book will help capture the sense of occasion as well as the flavour of the formative years of one of the world's greatest countries.*

*Embodying the true spirit of the Bicentennial celebrations the exhibition will, after its showing in London, make a grand tour of Australia visiting 7 venues in 16 months. We wish **First Impressions** well in the South Land, and its audiences great enjoyment.*

Dr Ron Hedley CB DSc
Director,
British Museum (Natural History)

A Flemish astrolobe c. 1570
SM

Chapter 1
European exploration of the Pacific 1520–1700

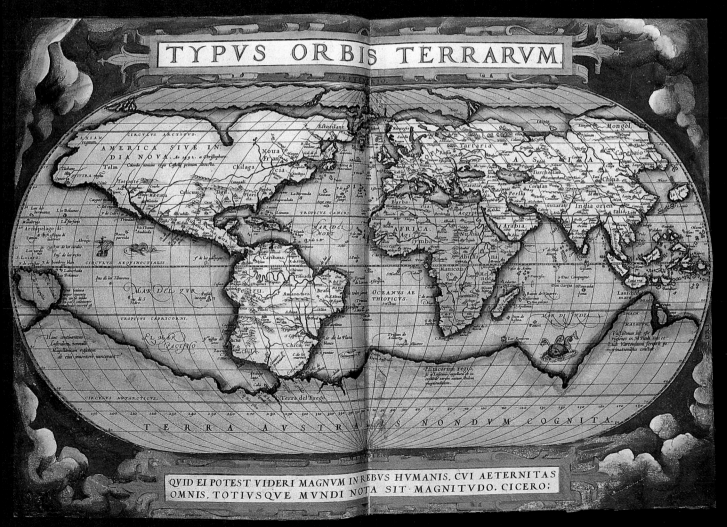

World map showing the Great South Land,
Terra Australis, by Ortelius, 1570.

Until as late as the middle of the 18th century the southern hemisphere appeared on all European maps as the seat of a great continent about which almost nothing was known. For centuries its possible existence had been left to the curiosity of the philosophers. The origin of the belief in its reality dated back to the Greeks and Romans whose geographers and philosophers argued on purely theoretical grounds that some such land must exist in the ocean of the southern hemisphere. Because of this conviction, Ptolemy the Geographer, writing in about AD150-60, had actually sketched in a huge area of land on the map. To it he gave the name 'Terra Australis', the South Land.

Ptolemy's maps survived to influence thinking and to be accepted by many geographers in the second half of the 16th century. Ortelius showed it quite clearly and Mercator also included it on his map, arguing that the South Land must indeed exist because its presence was necessary to balance the land masses in the northern hemisphere.

However, there were many practical reasons that prevented the solving of this mystery. Early navigators were pioneers gradually exploring and charting unknown seas. Before Ferdinand Magellan circumnavigated the world in 1522, proving it to be round, sailing beyond the horizon took great courage. Magellan passed

beyond Cape Horn for the first time, and entered the Southern Ocean through the strait that now bears his name. His course did not take him south towards the unknown continent, but further voyages helped to keep interest alive, and it was accepted that there was a problem of great importance awaiting solution. Did the continent really exist and, if so, what was its character and extent?

It is highly likely that navigators from many lands may have sighted the unnamed continent without leaving any record. Perhaps some discoveries were accidental, for the force of the prevailing winds alone may have brought early explorers in contact with the Australian coast. Many,

The Dauphin Map showing Java la Grande – one of several produced around 1536.
BM

however, in what was then a vast oceanic desert, did not survive shipwreck.

Before Magellan, the Portuguese Bartholomew Diaz had already given an impetus to voyages eastwards when he rounded the Cape of Good Hope in 1488. Meanwhile, European interest in this unexplored area of the globe varied from age to age, affected by the hard-won growth of knowledge and the needs of the time. Philosophical curiosity gradually gave way to the increasing pressures of the struggle for commercial and political supremacy that led to empire-building beyond Europe. Consequently, the politics of Europe often affected the way in which advancing knowledge could be used and further exploration pioneered. The results of voyages were sometimes suppressed for State reasons.

Early maps raise the possibility that Portuguese ships sailed close to Australian shores over 400 years ago. By the middle of the 16th century ships from rival nations were penetrating the Southern Ocean more and more frequently, drawn by the rich spice trade of the East Indies, but also penetrating northwards to China and Japan. Whether any of them sailed sufficiently far southwards to touch Australia is still open to conjecture. A well-known series of maps made in the French port of Dieppe between 1536 and 1567 suggest that they might have. The earliest of these maps was made by an unknown cartographer but uses Portuguese place names. This map shows Sumatra and Java in the East Indies separated by a narrow strait from a large land mass to the south. This land is named 'Java la Grande' and its shape, size and position correspond roughly to that of Australia. Such an early definition of the shape of Java la Grande corresponding with the north, and possibly the west, coast of Australia is puzzling. It has been suggested that this knowledge may have been passed to the Portuguese by Malay seamen, who have left evidence of their early presence on the northern coasts of Australia.

In the early 17th century Spain came very close to making a significant discovery. In 1606 Fernandez de Quiros,

entering the Southern Ocean by way of Cape Horn, came across an island in the New Hebrides group. In the name of the King of Spain he took immediate possession of what he thought was part of the Great South Land. Anticipating further discovery he claimed,

. . . all the lands which I sighted and am going to sight, and of all this region of the south as far as the Pole, which from this time shall be called Austrialia del Espiritu Santo, with all its dependencies and belongings.

Quiros returned to Spain to raise support for further exploration. In one of innumerable memoranda to his unresponsive monarch, he appealed for help on the grounds that

. . . it appears clearly that there are two large portions of the Earth severed from this of Europe, Africa and Asia. The first is America which Christopher Colon discovered; and the second and last of the world is that which I have seen and solicit to people and completely discover for your Majesty.

After years of delay he finally was able to set out again in 1614, only to die at Panama before he could complete his quest.

The first recorded European landfalls on the Australian mainland were made by the Dutch. It was after their arrival in the Pacific that Dutch ships began deliberately to solve the mystery of the likely presence of a southern continent. After Houtman

A caravel, c.1600,
the type of vessel used by
Dutch navigators to reach the
west coast of New Holland.

reached Java in 1596 by way of the Cape of Good Hope, Dutch ships were drawn to the East Indies in such numbers that they provided serious competition to the Spaniards. The Dutch East India Company was founded in 1602, 7 years before it actually secured the right from Spain to send its ships to trade in the Indies. In 1619 the Dutch Company founded its headquarters at Batavia (Jakarta), which was to be the centre of a Dutch colonial empire in the East. With the exception of the members of the Company, there was still a prohibition on the ships of any country sailing in these waters imposed by a powerful Spain.

So, the actual discovery of Australia fell to the Dutch, now in a position to explore the Southern Ocean. But, even before they had gained the right to be in the area, William Janszoon in the *Duyfken* had touched at New Guinea, then sailed further south to the Gulf of Carpentaria on the northern shores of Australia. Janszoon followed its eastern shore as far as Cape Keerweer (Turn Again) believing it to be connected to New Guinea. By the middle of the century the Dutch had charted and named sections of the north and south-west coasts of a land mass they named 'New Holland'. In 1642 and 1644 Abel Tasman made two important and wide-ranging

expeditions in an attempt to discover whether New Holland was part of the still elusive great southern continent. He also intended to discover if the equally mysterious New Guinea was an island or whether at some part it was connected with New Holland.

Tasman sailed south-east from Mauritius as far as what is now Tasmania. He named it Van Diemen's Land but was prevented from thoroughly examining his discovery by his crew's fear of the giants they believed must inhabit the island. Tasman then sailed further east to discover New Zealand, after which he returned northwards to New Guinea. Though

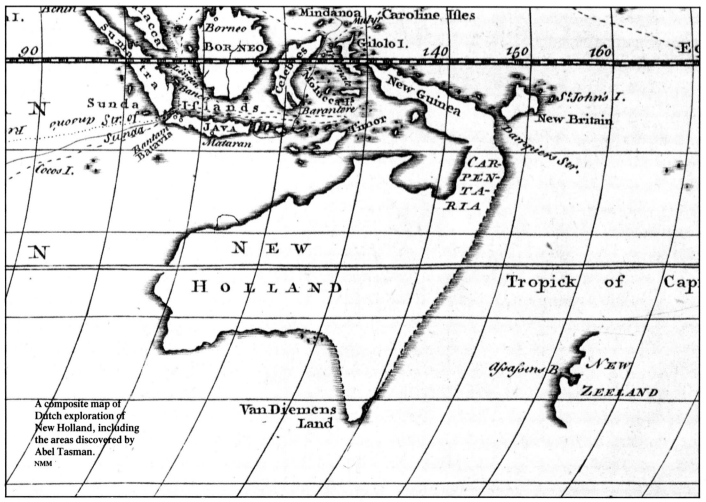

A composite map of Dutch exploration of New Holland, including the areas discovered by Abel Tasman.
NMM

Tasman had, in effect, 'sailed round Australia without seeing it', his tracks had further defined and limited the area available for a southern continent. Tasman's explorations were to be unsurpassed for over a century, until the voyages of James Cook.

In the interval the Dutch by no means abandoned their interests in the area though further exploration lost much of its impetus while Holland slid into serious political complications in Europe. Occasional Dutch ships found none of the exploitable trade resources that would have allowed them to justify the expense of organized exploration, but they continued to assemble information about those parts of the coastline with which they came in contact. By 1678 they had charted the north-west of Australia and from the North-West Cape to Cape Leveque.

The Dutch sometimes noted the wildlife of these areas and left the first manuscript record of the kangaroo or wallaby (1629). When Willem de Vlamingh explored the west coast of the continent and its Swan River in 1696, he raised perhaps the first controversy over its exotic fauna by his description of the black swans he found there. A letter from a Dutch correspondent to an English physician-naturalist concerning this voyage was published by the Royal Society, London, in 1698. It summed up almost as much as was known by this time of the country and its wildlife,

The soil of this country is very barren and like a desert; no freshwater rivers have been found, but some of salt-water; no quadrupeds, except one as large as a dog, with long ears, that lives in the water, as well as on the land. Black swans, parrots, and many sea-cows were found there.

Some of the descriptions of animals that had come back from these voyages were beyond imagination and early European explorers had no idea of what they would find in Australia. Tales of mythical beasts from foreign lands were not only common, but also more or less expected. They enjoyed credence in an ignorant and superstitious age. They were often seized on as a useful embellishment by frustrated map-makers faced with empty spaces on their maps. Jonathon Swift mocked these geographers who,

With savage pictures fill their gaps,
And o'er unhabitable downs
Place elephants for want of towns.

The first English vessel to visit the Australian coast was the *Cygnet* in 1688, exactly 100 years before European settlement. On board was William Dampier (1652-1715) who as a young man 'given to rambling' had left his employment on a Jamaican sugar plantation to go to sea 'in very mixed company'. He had been to both sides of Central America on trading and privateering ventures before he joined a group of buccaneers bound for the South Seas. Always somewhat detached from the desperate circumstances of which he was often a part, Dampier was insatiably curious about his world, and uninhibited in his pursuit of information, 'The further we went the more knowledge and experience I should get . . . which was the main thing I regarded' he wrote, ingenuously explaining his occupation.

The *Cygnet* sailed into the Pacific by way of Cape Horn and spent some time on the Australian coast in and around King Sound after a landfall at Cape Leveque. It returned to England in 1691 after various experimental trading escapades that took it to parts of South East Asia, the Philippines, New Guinea and the islands of the eastern archipelago. Dampier published a vivid account of this journey, *A New Voyage round the World* (London 1697), written up from notes he had preserved carefully in waterproof bamboo cylinders sealed with wax.

William Dampier (1651–1751), navigator and adventurer, the first Englishman to reach Australia. By Thomas Murray, oil on canvas.
NPG

His book was so successful he was sought out by men of culture and influence. He met Pepys and Evelyn, and members of the powerful Royal Society, its president Charles Montague (to whom he had dedicated his book) and its secretary Sir Hans Sloane. Dampier was quickly recognized as a possible authority on the mysterious South Seas and Montague introduced him to the First Lord of the Admiralty (Edward Russell, Earl of Orford). After he had been consulted by the Admiralty, plans emerged for Dampier to go on an exploring expedition 'wherein I might be serviceable to my Nation'. Delighted, he proposed to set out for 'the remoter part of the East India Islands and the neighbouring Coast of Terra Australis', to solve the riddle of the southern continent, for, as he wrote, 'there is no larger tract of land hitherto undiscovered' whether 'a continued land or not'.

On this ambitious quest Dampier left England in January 1699 in command of HMS *Roebuck* (290 tons) with a crew of 50 men. He had only one ship instead of the two he had asked for and fewer supplies than he had calculated he would need. After frustrating delays, he also had to abandon his original plan to sail westward by Cape Horn to northern New Holland and New Guinea (as Cook was to do in 1770) and went by the Cape of Good Hope. A brief stop was necessary at Brazil to off-load an insubordinate naval officer. On 1 August 1699 the *Roebuck* made a landfall near the Houtman Abrolhos group of islands off the west coast of Australia. Dampier was unable to find an anchorage until 5 days later at an inlet on the Australian coast he named Shark Bay. Searching for supplies and water he bore north, intending to return south later.

The *Roebuck* followed the north-west coastline of the continent for 5 weeks while Dampier made notes and collected specimens of plants, which were pressed between the pages of books to dry. In that early springtime he found 'besides some Plants, Herbs, and tall Flowers, some very small flowers, growing on the Ground, that were sweet and beautiful, and for the most part unlike any I had seen elsewhere'. Whether intentionally or accidentally, he had on board 'a Person Skill'd in Drawing' who sketched the birds, fishes and animals that could not be preserved. Dampier added his own written descriptions to these drawings. The expedition found few land animals, most of which interested a hungry crew only as a source of food, but there were snakes, lizards and an abundance of fishes. Dampier ingeniously described the first kangaroos or wallabies he saw as '. . . a sort of Racoons' different, he thought, to those he had seen in the West Indies 'for these have very short Fore-legs; but go jumping upon them as the others do . . .'

Dampier's reliable impression of the west coast of Australia was of a long series of reefs and shoals behind which lay sandhills and barren country, inhabited as far as he could determine from no contact by, 'the miserablest People in the World'.

Place this P. 123.

F. 3.

A Noddy. of N. Holland. P. 123 & 143.

F. 5.

The head & greatest part of ye neck of this bird is red, & therein differs from the Avosetta of Italy.

A Comon Noddy. P. 143

F. 6.

F. 4.

The Bill & Leggs of this Bird are of a Bright Red.

Birds of New Holland, drawn by a member of Dampier's crew and published in *A voyage to New Holland* (1703).
BL

Hampered by the difficult sailing conditions, lack of fresh water and a restless crew, 'heartless enough to the Voyage at the best', Dampier left the Australian coast near Roebuck Bay (the present Dampier Archipelago) in September 1699. He set his course for Timor then went east towards the north coast of New Guinea where he sighted and named New Britain. The urgent need to repair the *Roebuck* forced him to return to the Dutch port of Batavia. There the condition of the ship was so bad that he had to abandon his intended explorations and never reached the east coast of Australia. On the homeward voyage the unreliable *Roebuck* finally foundered at Ascension island but sluggishly enough to allow Dampier to save his records and specimens.

After surviving the regulation court-martial for losing his ship but being fined the whole of his pay, Dampier published the journal of his expedition and its sketches as *A Voyage to New Holland* (London 1703). This book provided the first published account of the plants and animals of Australia in graphic form and shows the attention that Dampier had given to natural history. One of the flowers in his collection, the wattle, was to become an Australian national emblem. The original specimens he brought back with him are now held by the University of Oxford.

The South Seas lured Dampier into two further voyages, but in the meantime he had become immensely popular as an author, and his books were reprinted many times. The absence of 'the most distant appearance of invention' in his writing began a vogue in travel literature that fed readers for a century and influenced some of the great works of English literature. In 1726 Jonathan Swift published his classic *Gulliver's Travels,* a novel about 'a person of quality in Terra Australis Incognita'. This parody of a South Sea voyage set its scenes in the North Pacific or off New Holland and showed the connection was deliberate by having Gulliver refer to 'my cousin Dampier'. Daniel Defoe wrote no fewer than eight stories under the strong influence of Dampier's accounts and produced his own entirely fictitious *New Voyage round the World.*

Despite his enduring literary associations, Dampier's narratives enjoy a further significance. As an acute, scientific observer he was well ahead of his time in 'his intense devotion to the gathering, assessment, and recording of . . . natural and social phenomena'. Fascinated with the precise observation of the world, its elements and its multitudinous forms of life, he anticipates the need to systematize that is the mark of the men of the 18th century. His own description of the winds and currents of the Pacific *Discourse of Trade Winds* (1699) still has the respect of navigators and meteorologists. Dampier's books helped to give substance and impetus to popular curiosity about the southern continent. The next phase of exploration of Australia by his fellow countrymen was to be characterized by this same sober, critical curiosity.

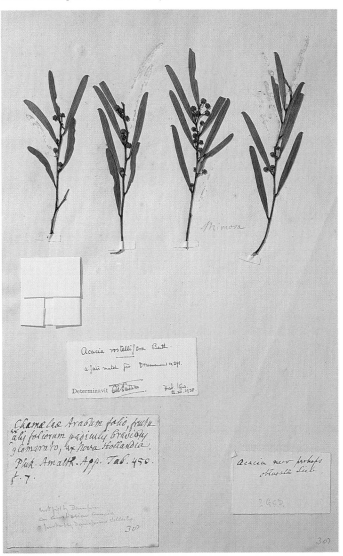

Wattle *Acacia rostellifera* collected by Dampier on the Australian west coast and salvaged when the *Roebuck* sank off Ascension Island.
FDH

13

Route of the *Endeavour* (1768–71).

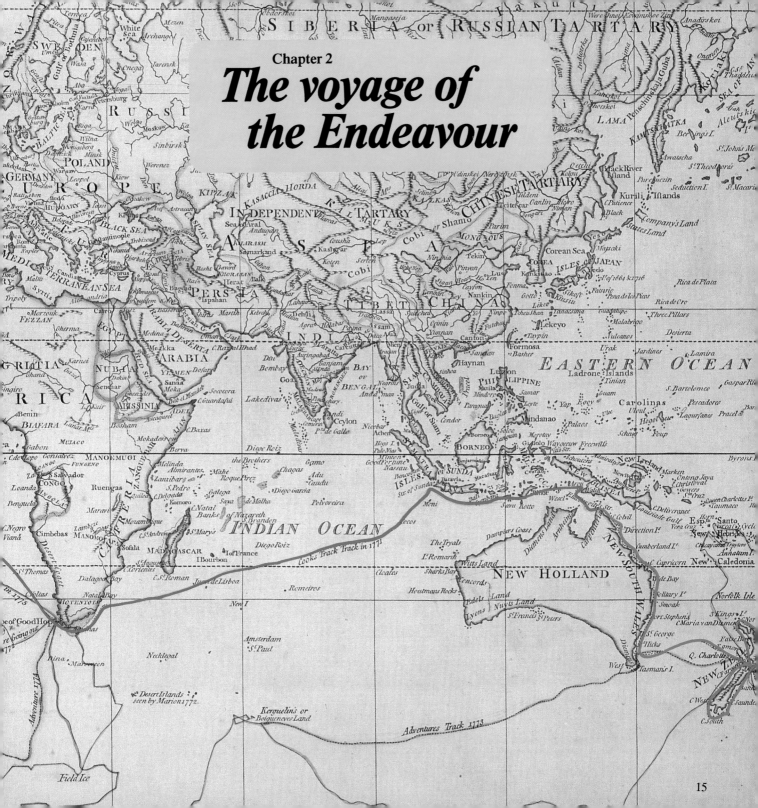

By the middle of the 18th century European activity in the Pacific or South Seas had become persistent. Spain's rich colonial empire had always been a source of frustration and envy to its rivals. Spain's competitors had been gathering strength and her empire was beginning to be seen as 'a great and undeveloped estate with important frontages on the Pacific'. The conviction that this empire was 'soon to come on the market' encouraged interest in the Pacific. Further encouragement came from a dawning concern with science and geography, promoted in England by the Royal Society and the Admiralty. Successive voyages were made by the English into the Spanish dominated Pacific, after a daring foray by Admiral Anson in the early 1740s. Anson's raid was the first deliberate challenge to Spain's claim to monopoly of the area. Essentially concerned with commercial opportunity, he urged that settlements be made at strategic points in the Pacific to supply and service British shipping.

Anson's vision did not ignore the possibility of discovering the Great South Land. If it should turn out to offer commercial opportunity to any country that could discover and acquire it, so much the better. The French too, made frequent exploratory voyages in the region in the early 18th century, the most notable by Bougainville in 1767-69. The Frenchman, Charles de Brosses, asserted in his *Histoire des Navigations aux Terres Australies* (1757) that the unravelling of this Pacific mystery would be 'the grandest, noblest, most useful enterprise a sovereign could undertake'. The Spanish had neglected easy opportunities to explore the Pacific from their colonial settlements in South America, being content to exploit the easy wealth of their bullion mines. Though the French were also deeply curious it was, as de Brosses feared, the British who pursued the question with growing determination.

In 1764 Commodore John Byron left England with orders to search for any unknown lands in the South Atlantic. He followed his instructions to take possession of the Falkland Islands group and search for a North West Passage on the north-west coast of America before returning by way of the Pacific. Byron, however, actually spent most of his time in the Pacific and the Admiralty sent another expedition out in 1766, only months after his return. This expedition, under Captain Samuel Wallis in the *Dolphin,* took possession of Tahiti in 1767. Access to Tahiti changed the nature of Pacific exploration, providing an invaluable base for future expeditions into this formidable 'desert of oceans'.

The exploration of the east (Pacific) coast of Australia began to owe less and less to chance circumstances or to prevailing winds. On 26 August 1768 Lieutenant James Cook (1728-1779), 'with a reputation for accuracy and skill in charting' gained through long experience, sailed from Plymouth in command of the ship *Endeavour* (368 tons) on the first of his three legendary expeditions to the Pacific. This historic voyage took nearly 3 years. In the course of it Cook mapped over 5000 miles of the east coast of Australia.

Shortly before the return of Captain Samuel Wallis in 1767, the Royal Society had petitioned King George III for support in arrangements for a scientific expedition to the south Seas to observe the transit of the planet Venus, due to occur in 1769. From these measurements it was hoped to estimate the distance between the Sun and the Earth which would advance the accuracy of navigation. The King contributed £4000 and the Admiralty prepared a ship to send to the newly discovered island of Tahiti. Also at the Royal Society's request a small group of civilian scientists was added. At his own

James Cook (1728–79) explorer and navigator. By Nathanial Dance, oil on canvas.
NMM

expense, one of their members, Joseph Banks (1743-1820) and some of his associates accompanied the expedition to record all aspects of the strange new world.

After a change of name from the *Earl of Pembroke* to the *Endeavour,* a three-masted coal ship from Whitby was fitted and rigged out at Deptford Dock. Like all coal boats the *Endeavour* was extremely strongly built and easy to refloat if grounded. She was also roomy enough to stow the stores needed for such a long voyage, the salt provisions, drinking water and coal for ovens. No expense was spared in alterations and repairs. An extra deck was added to accommodate all the crew. Wooden planks and sheathing were fixed to the hull and the gap created between was filled with nails to protect the ship against wood-eating ship worms. Thirty metres long and less than 10 metres wide, she was armed with 10 fixed guns and 12 swivels and 'twelve of His Majesty's marines, assigned to protect the crew from savages'.

The ship's company was chosen carefully. It included Lieutenant Zachary Hicks, Lieutenant John Gore who had twice already circumnavigated the world, including once with Wallis in the *Dolphin.* The master and his two mates had also served under Wallis. There was a surgeon, a carpenter, a gunner and a clerk. The remainder of the crew consisted of a cook, a steward, two quartermasters, an armourer, a sailmaker, three midshipmen, 41 able seamen and nine servants. Ninety-four people with their stores, livestock and two dogs boarded the *Endeavour.*

The choice of her commander had been no less careful. Cook received his commission on the 26 May 1768 and the following day went aboard the *Endeavour,* hoisted the pennant and took charge. A tall impressive man with 'an agreeable modesty' Cook was well-liked and respected by his crew. An air of austerity did not disguise his capacity, and though a man of action rather than reflection his conversation was lively and intelligent.

Forty-year-old Cook, from a large Yorkshire family, had enjoyed no advantages in life and had made his own fortune steadily by application and talent.

From the Merchant Marines he had entered the Royal Navy as master's mate. Cook had shown his mettle and gained a reputation in the recent war with the French in Canada. He took part in the siege of Louisburg. His had been the dangerous task of surveying the St Lawrence River, under attack from the French shore batteries and marauding Indians. It was Cook's charts that had guided the British fleet before Wolfe captured Quebec. After the war Cook had been employed in surveying the coasts of Nova Scotia and Newfoundland. Impressed by his work and his published maps, the Royal Society appointed him one of their official observers for the transit of Venus. The other observer was Charles Green, assistant to the Astronomer Royal.

Much secrecy had surrounded the preparation of the ship at Plymouth, giving rise to a rumour, strenuously denied, that Cook had sealed orders to be opened after he left Tahiti. These orders were expected to launch a voyage of discovery which, as the *London Gazette* speculated,

. . . will carry Endeavour to lands far distant in the Pacific (south), and even to that vast continent which is said to be quite as big as Europe and Asia together, and which is now marked on the Maps as Terra Australis Nondum Cognita.

In summarising the ultimate destination of the *Endeavour* the *Gazette* accurately observed that the *Endeavour* carried 'every chart book and scrap of evidence relative to the Pacific Ocean' and added that 'it was no secret' that the Royal Society's original choice for commander, Alexander Dalrymple, had given Joseph Banks a mysterious document containing the statement of the Spanish captain, Luis Vaez de Torres, 'that he had sailed between two great land masses in the far South' more than 150 years earlier. The newspaper was equally confident that Cook was to claim any 'unhabited Countries' as well as assess 'the number

Inhabitants of the island of Tierra del Fuego. By Alexander Buchan. BL

and disposition of the Natives, and to cultivate a friendship and alliance with them.'

On such a long and uncertain voyage the general state of health was a practical consideration for there was no chance of replacing crew. In an attempt to prevent a disabling outbreak of scurvy it was usual to supplement supplies at sea with fishes, and with fruit and livestock at various landfalls. A goat was carried on board the *Endeavour* to provide fresh milk for the officers, an experiment that had been pioneered successfully on the *Dolphin*. The goat survived the voyage and had a couplet composed in Latin to its fame, by Dr Johnson. Large quantities of fresh citrus juice were carried in kegs and drunk neat when any sign of scurvy appeared. Preserved cabbage or sauerkraut and sea celery soup were provided to augment the salted meat and weeviled ship's biscuits that were the regular diet.

A tupapow in the Island of Otaheite. By Sydney Parkinson.
BL

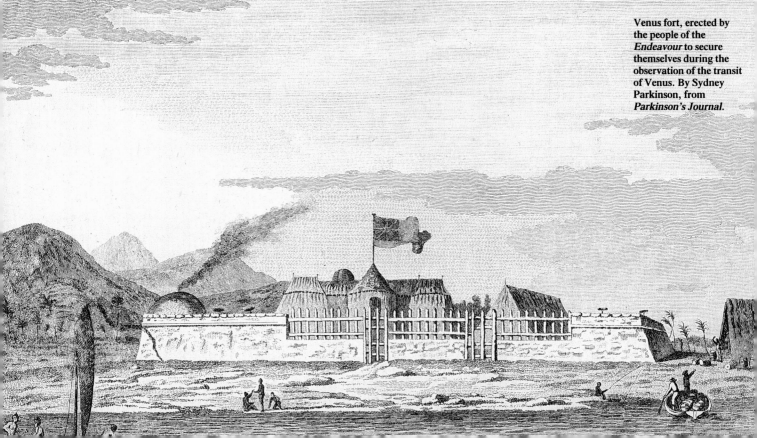

Venus fort, erected by the people of the *Endeavour* to secure themselves during the observation of the transit of Venus. By Sydney Parkinson, from *Parkinson's Journal*.

When Cook found that the crew at first would not eat the sauerkraut, he tried a new approach, but one he had never known to fail. He had the sauerkraut served at the officers' table daily and left it to the option of the seamen to take as much as they pleased. As he wrote with some satisfaction in his journal,

This practice was not continued above a week before I found it necessary to put everyone on board on an allowance; for such are the tempers and disposition of seamen in general, that whatever you give them out of the common way, although it be ever so much for their good, it will not go down and you will hear nothing but murmurings against the men that first invented it; but the moment they see their superiors set a value upon it, it becomes the finest stuff in the world and the inventor an honest fellow. Wind Easterly.

The *Endeavour* sailed into the Pacific by way of Cape Horn and reached Tahiti in April 1769. With 3 months in hand to prepare for the transit of Venus on 3 June a temporary fort was built on a sandy beach, within range of the ship's guns. Inside the fort were set up the observation equipment and tent. Meanwhile charting the islands and collecting natural history specimens, and replenishing the stores, occupied everyone. On 3 June though the sky was clear the results of the observation were disappointing, as a dense cloud around the planet ruined all chance of taking accurate measurements.

His task at Tahiti completed, Cook opened his secret instructions. They confirmed that he was to attempt to solve the problem of the existence of a southern continent. Cook knew only that, like several pieces of a jigsaw, coastlines had been sighted to the north (New Guinea) of any supposed continent, to the east (New Zealand), to the south (Van Diemen's Land) and to the west (western Australia). It was his task to discover whether these pieces belonged to the same picture. Accordingly he sailed south towards New Zealand, circumnavigated both its islands, charted its coasts and took formal possession. He then made the decision to steer 'to the Westward until we fall in with the E. coast of New Holland'.

A view in New Zealand.
By Sydney Parkinson.
BL

Maori face.
By Sydney Parkinson.
BL

19

The mainland of Australia was sighted near its south-eastern tip (Point Hicks) at 6 pm on 19 April 1770 by Lieutenant Zachary Hicks. The *Endeavour* was to be on its coast for the next 5 months. Sailing northward in search of an anchorage, Cook sighted and entered a large tranquil bay on 29 April 1770 where the ship remained for a week. Cook had called this first anchorage Stingray Bay because of the great number of rays that were caught, including the biggest which was over 150 kilograms, but he later changed the name to Botanists Bay, and finally to Botany Bay.

He continued northwards charting the coast for 5 weeks, landing at Bustard Bay and Cape Townshend at the southern end of the Great Barrier Reef, of which he was then unaware, and sailing closer to the land than he would have preferred in order to make accurate observations. By June the *Endeavour* was within the Barrier Reef amidst coral and dangerous shoals. Still creeping north, taking careful soundings and often preceded by the long-boat, they reached Trinity Bay (Cairns) whose

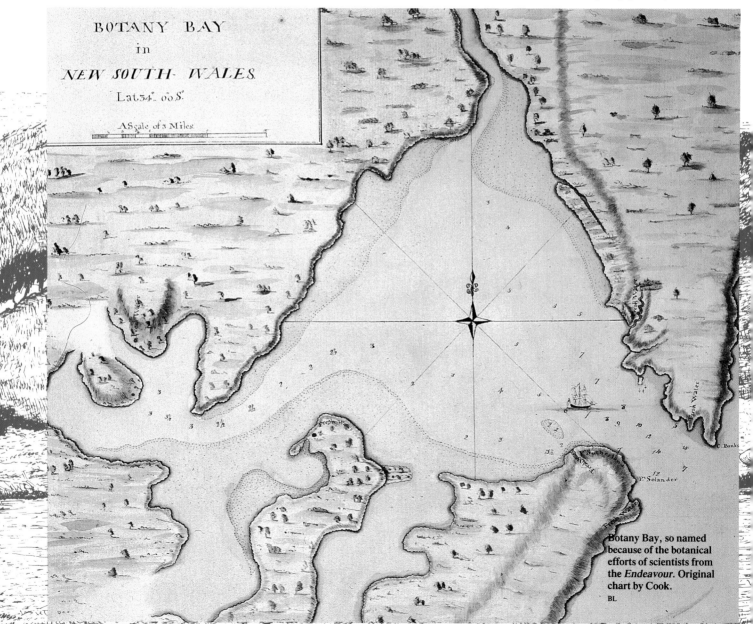

BOTANY BAY in NEW SOUTH WALES. Lat 34°. 00 S. A Scale of 3 Miles.

Botany Bay, so named because of the botanical efforts of scientists from the *Endeavour*. Original chart by Cook.
BL

northern point Cook named Tribulation Bay, for, he wrote, 'Here began all our troubles.'

The hazards of their progress had been clear to everyone. It was probably no surprise when on 11 June the *Endeavour* 'struck and stuck fast' on a coral reef. It was 12 hours before the ship, lightened by abandoning all moveables, was hauled off the reef with windlass and anchors. With a gaping hole and with pumps working constantly it took 3 days to find a safe place before the ship could be beached at the mouth of the Endeavour River (now Cooktown) for repair. Gales hampered the work for 7 weeks.

Joseph Banks and his companions previously had been able to make only brief collecting trips but they now had the opportunity for extensive collecting. Banks organized a 3-day expedition up the Endeavour River and on this trip they got closer to the native aboriginals than at any other time. Previously the aboriginals had kept out of reach, though their camp fires on shore had often been sighted from the ship, especially at one place Cook had named Smoky Cape. Though the aboriginals were interested in the turtles offered them, they showed no interest in gaudy gifts and seemed to Cook 'to wish nothing more than that we should be gone'.

Cook satisfied himself about the accuracy of Dampier's observations on the Australian aboriginal, that they had no houses, no skin garments, sheep, poultry and fruits of the earth. However, he argued eloquently that this was no drawback because,

They live in a Tranquillity which is not disturbed by the Inequality of Condition. The Earth and sea of their own accord furnishes them with all things necessary for life, they covet not magnificent Houses, House-hold Staff etc., they live in a warm and fine climate and enjoy a very wholesome Air, so that they have very little need of Clothing.

Furthermore, Cook pointed out, the fact that the aboriginals set no value on the things offered them, often abandoning them carelessly, confirmed that they 'think themselves provided with all the necessaries

Beached for repair at Endeavour River.

'Two natives of New Holland advancing to combat.' Engraving after Parkinson's sketch of two aboriginals seen on the beach at Botany Bay.
BM(NH)

of Life . . . ' Perhaps influenced by a seaman's self-reliance and economy, Cook was able to appreciate the simplicity of the aboriginal way of life. 'In reality', he stated firmly,

. . . they are far happier than we Europeans; being wholly unacquainted not only with the superflous but the necessary Conveniences so much sought after in Europe, they are happy in not knowing the use of them.

When the *Endeavour* was able to take to sea again, Cook 'was at a loss to know which way to sail' to reach the open sea to the east. Tensely they searched for a break in the outer reef. The opening they found and through which they escaped is known today as 'Cook's Passage'. Their escape was not complete, however, for 2 days later a sudden change of wind and huge waves drove the ship towards a wall of coral rock rising almost perpendicularly out of the water. 'All the dangers we had escaped were little in comparison of being thrown upon this reef, where the ship must be dashed to pieces in a moment' wrote Cook. When the *Endeavour* was only a wave's breadth from doom a tiny intermittent breeze decisively balanced their desperate attempts to tow the ship in a slanting direction across the face of the reef. Still in danger Cook took the ship landwards again through Providential Channel, and decided to hug the shore and remain inside the reef while they sailed towards the northern extremity of the continent.

On 22 August 1770 Cook landed on a small island at the tip of Cape York. There Cook hoisted the flag and took possession of the whole of the eastern coast of Australia, later giving it the name 'New South Wales' in his journal. He called this place Possession Island.

On his progress up the eastern coast Cook had been impressed by the many beautiful coastal regions, naming their features after influential people in public life in England. Many places still bear these names. Cook found 'this Eastern side is not that barren and miserable country that Dampier and others have described the western side to be'. As he wrote in his journal,

The Coast of the Country, at least so much of it as lays to the Northward of 25° of Latitude, abounds with a great number of fine bays and harbours . . . In this extensive Country it can never be doubted but what most sorts of grains, fruit, roots etc. of every kind would flourish here once brought hither, planted and Cultivated by the hands of Industry.

After leaving Possession Island, Cook intended to establish whether there was indeed a passage separating Australia from New Guinea and he went on to find and name Endeavour Strait at the north of the continent. This task completed, he made a final landfall at Booby Island before anchoring at Batavia for repairs and supplies. In this notorious death-trap for seamen, malaria and dysentery ravaged the *Endeavour*. 'We came here with as healthy a ship's company as need go to sea' wrote Cook bitterly, 'and after a stay of not quite

three months left in the condition of a Hospital Ship, besides the loss of 7 men.' On the return voyage to the Cape of Good Hope 23 more of the crew were buried at sea. From the Cape the *Endeavour* returned to England in company with an East India Fleet, and anchored on 15 July 1771.

Two years later the story of this magnificent achievement was published in a badly garbled form as *An Account of the Voyages undertaken by his present Majesty for making Discoveries in the Southern Hemisphere, drawn up from the Journals which were kept by the several Commanders and from the Papers of Joseph Banks, Esq.* It was published in three volumes and compiled, in the absence of Cook, by John Hawkesworth. Cook's own detailed and vivid journal was not published for another century.

Cook had little further contact with the Australian continent. During his next voyage (1772), intended to settle finally the question of the existence of any other southern continent, his companion ship the *Adventure,* while separated from Cook's ship *Resolution,* anchored off an island on the south-east coast of Tasmania (Adventure Bay). Her captain, Tobias Furneaux, made a sketch now regarded as the first known landscape of Tasmania. Several birds shot there were taken to New Zealand where George Forster made pencil sketches that are now in the Banks Collection of the British Museum (Natural History). On his third voyage Cook also anchored at Adventure Bay in January 1777 on his way to New Zealand and Tahiti.

Cook, 'the supreme navigator of the 18th century', did more than anyone else of his time to extend European knowledge of the geography of other countries. His voyages sketched in the missing boundaries of the lands of the Southern Ocean and solved a puzzle that had been debated since men first started making maps. Cook's activity in these previously uncharted parts of the world and the accuracy of his mapping unlocked the door to the Pacific and to European colonization of the South Pacific. The process began with the exploration of Australia.

Chapter 3
The Royal Society
and the Endeavour

The young Joseph Banks (1743–1820). By Joshua Reynolds, oil on canvas. NPG

The voyage of the *Endeavour* began the systematic investigation of the world's fifth and last continent. Thanks to the intervention of the Royal Society, Cook's voyage was marked not only by the discovery of new lands but also by the flood of information it returned with about the natural world. The impact of this first contact with a continent apparently so undisturbed and with living systems so different and so'new altered the course of scientific thinking. The result stimulated fascination and intellectual delight as well as increasing controversy and disturbing accepted patterns of thinking.

Scientists, naturalists and artists on board the *Endeavour* brought back the first detailed descriptions of plants and animals on the east coast of the Australian continent. Some of the specimens they took back to England over 200 years ago are still in existence. For decades these specimens and the drawings and paintings they made, which today are primarily of historical interest, were regarded as instructive and living material, and were almost the only way people could extend their knowledge of Australia.

Despite the primary concern of the British Admiralty with exploration, thanks to the presence of the wealthy Joseph Banks, the *Endeavour* was to become a floating scientific institution. The general public first learned of Banks's involvement from a note in the *London Gazette* which announced that

The Royal Society has appointed its representative body of scientists and naturalists, led by the brilliant Botanist, Mr Joseph Banks. Mr Banks is paying his own expenses on the voyage also those expenses of his assistants and servants. The Second-in-Command is Mr Daniel Solander, a knowledgeable student of Natural History. Mr Alexander Buchan and Mr Sidney Parkinson have been engaged to 'sketch' views and plants.

Joseph Banks (1743-1820), a Lincolnshire landowner, was to become one of the most significant and influential figures of his time. Well-educated and enterprising, he had begun to devote his resources to the study of botany from an early age. By the time he was 20 he had already been on a botanizing and exploring voyage to the North Sea with his lifelong naval friend Constantine Phipps, later Lord Mulgrave, and on his return had become a Fellow of the Royal Society in 1766. The following year Banks spent 6 months in Newfoundland at the same time as James Cook was occupied in charting its coastline.

After the Royal Society had approved the appointment of its party on the *Endeavour,* the rest of the arrangements seem to have been left very much in Banks's own hands. It was usual at the time for young men of his wealth and cultivated background to explore the world on a Grand Tour of Europe usually accompanied by a tutor or artist. Banks was to out-do them all. On board the *Endeavour* he took a party of seven, including naturalists and natural history artists. His intention was not only to preserve a methodical record of the plant life but also to bring back descriptions of what, after all, was a great adventure. He hoped to entertain his friends on his return with revelations about new countries and their inhabitants and also make a contribution to scientific curiosity.

The party Banks was responsible for recruiting consisted of two Swedes, the botanist Daniel Carl Solander and Herman Dietrich Spöring. Spöring was Banks's secretary, Sydney Parkinson and fellow Scot Alexander Buchan were to record natural history subjects, and in Buchan's case to make pictorial records. Banks also took with him two volunteers from his

Daniel Solander (1733–82), botanist and taxonomist. By Johann Zoffany, oil on canvas.
LS

Lincolnshire estate with 'a tolerable notion of Natural History', James Roberts and Peter Briscoe, who were intended to assist the collectors. Two black servants, Thomas Richmond and J. Dorlington went also.

Daniel Solander (1733-1782) was granted absence from his post of assistant librarian at the British Museum (founded in 1753) where he had been cataloguing its natural history collection. Solander had studied under the great botanist Linnaeus, was a fellow of the Royal Society and was well known in scientific circles. He joined the *Endeavour* on an annual salary of £400 to help Banks order and catalogue the collection of natural history specimens to be made on the voyage. Short, jovial and plump, with a notorious weakness for elaborate waistcoats, he left with some reluctance to face the challenges of the expedition. His feelings were reciprocated by his friends: 'Everybody here parted from him with great reluctance, for no man was ever more beloved and in so great an esteem with the public from his affable and polite behaviour' wrote one of his acquaintances.

According to Solander, the voyage was to cost Banks the immense sum of £10 000. Certainly their equipment was lavish. 'No people ever went to sea better fitted out for the purpose of Natural History nor more elegantly' wrote one scholar, ' . . . they have all sorts of machines for catching and preserving insects; all kinds of nets, trawls, drags and hooks for coral fishing; they even have a curious contrivance of a telescope, by which, put under water, you can see the bottom at a great depth, where it is clear'. Space was found for a library of over a hundred books, including almost everything available in print about the natural history of the South Seas. There is no surviving evidence of the umbrellas suggested by one anxious friend who recommended 'both the silk French kind and the strong oilskin ones, also oilskin coats to guard against the torrents of rain you may expect'.

Young, confident and adventurous Banks was unlikely to worry about umbrellas. At Rio, during the early part of the voyage, the ship's company, who were suspected of being contraband traders by the Viceroy, were not allowed to land. Banks, in company with Solander and Sydney Parkinson, demonstrated a daredevil courage, slipping ashore at night to collect botanical specimens. The lists of these plants occupied 11 closely printed pages. The serious hazards of the expedition were brought home, however, when the *Endeavour* was rounding Cape Horn. At one of their landfalls Banks's company exploring ashore were suddenly engulfed in a snow blizzard and separated from one another. Young Alexander Buchan, who proved to be an epileptic, became ill and Solander had to be forcibly prevented from going to sleep in the snow. Banks's two servants succumbed to sleep and perished during the night.

Cook and Banks developed an early mutual respect, and after he had a chance to observe the methods of his unusual party Cook decided that 'Mr Banks and Dr Solander in natural history and other things useful to the learned world cannot fail to contribute very much to the success of the voyage.' To some extent these civilians must have been of help to him in carrying out his orders from the Admiralty which ran,

You are also to be careful to observe the nature of the soil and the products thereof, the beasts and fowls that inhabit or frequent it; the fishes that are to be found in the rivers or upon the coast, and in what plenty, and in case you find any mines, minerals or valuable stones, you are to bring home

Sydney Parkinson (1745–71), botanical artist. Probably a self portrait, in oils.
BM(NH)

27

specimens of each, as also such specimens of the seeds of trees, of fruits and grains as you may be able to collect, and transmit them to our Secretary that we may cause proper examination and experiments to be made of them. You are likewise to observe the genius, temper, disposition and number of the Natives.

As far as contact with other races was concerned Cook found Banks a great help and at all landfalls took him ashore with him. Banks showed no fear in these often tense situations, though he had proper caution, and seemed to be able to convey his own innocent curiosity to all groups of natives that they met.

Banks was able to begin serious botanizing at Tahiti but he found a variety of interesting activities. He was appointed by Cook to supervise all barter between the crews and Tahitians, under a strict set of regulations. Banks was soon in daily negotiations arranging for the revictualling of the ship and the replenishment of all stores, learning enough of the language in the exercise to make himself understood. Consequently 'Our traffick with this people' wrote Cook, 'was carried on with so much order as the best regulated market in Europe.' On their further journey to New Zealand, however, much of the livestock he had purchased in Tahiti perished in the increasing cold. On their first landing at New Zealand, Cook took Banks and Solander with him to attempt to make contact with the natives. Though the Maoris remained war-like and it was difficult to communicate at all, Banks was able to make an accurate and detailed description that convinced Cook of the Polynesian connections between their language and that of the Tahitians.

Above
Drumsticks
Isopogon anemonifolius,
collected at Botany Bay.
By Sydney Parkinson.
BM(NH)

Right
Grevilla pteridifolia,
collected at lookout point,
By Parkinson, completed
by J F Miller.

During the voyage the scientists usually spent the first half of the day studying with the aid of the books in their well-stocked library. Most of Banks's party had been familiar with one another before they had embarked. Spöring was Banks's secretary and Parkinson had already worked on Banks's collections. Solander must have been a great social asset on the *Endeavour*. An accomplished linguist, 'a philosophical gossip' and conversationalist, the great cabin must have benefitted, as did London society, from his presence. In moments of relaxation the group on the ship must have

presented a congenial focus. Banks, with his eager and lively mind tempered by an unusually sensitive response to other people, had chosen his travelling companions well.

At their first Australian landfall at Stingray Bay, Banks and Solander seized their opportunity, and while parties from the crew of the *Endeavour* sought fresh water, or went charting, the botanists collected. In only 6 days around the perimeter of the bay 3000 plant specimens, representing over 200 new species, were collected. Somewhat astonished at this

haul Cook changed his mind about the name of the bay and called it Botany Bay. He also named the northern and southern points of the bay Cape Banks and Cape Solander. On board the collectors sorted their specimens in the Great Cabin while Parkinson sketched the plants that were passed to him. In his journal Banks described how they worked together, 'From 4 to 5, when the cabin had lost the odour of food, we sat till dark by the great table with our draughtsman opposite and showed him in what way to make his drawings and ourselves made rapid

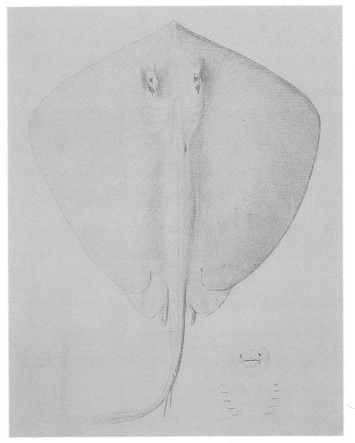

Left
Scarlet-flower blood-root
Haemodorum coccineum.
Collected at Endeavour River.
By Sydney Parkinson,
completed by J F Miller.
BM(NH)

Above
Stingray
Urolophus testaceus.
By Hermann Spöring.
BM(NH)

descriptions of all the details of natural history while our specimens were still fresh.' While they were at a landfall the industrious and conscientious Parkinson had to work at superhuman pace. The *Endeavour* left Botany Bay on 7 May 1770. Within 5 days of their departure Parkinson had finished 94 delicate and vivid sketches of plants from the Botany Bay collection.

The *Endeavour* was at Botany Bay for only a week. Alexander Buchan had died at Tahiti and his loss meant that Parkinson carried a double responsibility. Herman Spöring, who had some ability as a draughtsman, did his best to help and made drawings of some of the rays caught at Botany Bay. When the rays were appropriated by the cooks for food, Parkinson noted non-committally that they 'tasted very much like the European rays'.

As they were collected, plants were put in tin boxes, then taken on board the *Endeavour* where they were labelled and drawn. Some days so many specimens were gathered that they had to be preserved as fresh as possible between damp cloths, until Parkinson was ready to deal with them. Experiments had to be made constantly to discover the best way to preserve them. Fortunately Banks had thought to provide a huge store of drying paper, buying up 4800 unbound sheets of Milton's *Paradise Lost* before they left London.

Solander, too, was working at a constant pace. On land he collected with Banks. During the voyage they stored 30 382 specimens. In this collection they had 3607 different species of which some 1400 were entirely unknown. Solander spent the long days at sea describing and classifying these specimens. Using the system he had learned with Linnaeus he first organized the plants into genera, then meticulously described each specimen on a small card which was filed. At the end of the voyage he already had compiled 25 volumes of his cards for botanical specimens and 27 volumes for zoological specimens.

Despite the constant flow of work waiting for him, Parkinson took every opportunity to indulge his own real curiosity and 'ardent thirst after knowledge'. He clearly and carefully

recorded his own impressions in his journal. After landing at Botany Bay he wrote, 'The country is very level and fertile, the soil a kind of grey sand; and the climate mild: and though it was the beginning of winter when we arrived, everything seemed in perfection.' He had a close look at the vegetation, recording 'a variety of flowering shrubs; a tree that yields gum; and a species of palm, the berries of which are of two sorts: one small, eaten by the hogs, and the other, as large as a cherry, has a stone in it; it is of a pale crimson colour and has the taste of sweet acid. We also found a species of Salvia Fortia.'

The investigators found few signs of animals at their first landfall and had to be content to speculate on a quadruped 'about the size of a hare', the dung of a large animal that fed on grass and a cast-off snake skin. There was, however, a striking abundance of birds including brilliantly coloured parrots. Their beautiful plumage did not save them from being made into a pie. Parkinson gave honour where it was

due. 'They ate very well,' he observed before adding that 'We also met with a black bird, very much like our crow, and shot some of them too, which also tasted agreeably.' Ravens, quails and cockatoos were also sighted and they managed to trap a rainbow lorikeet, which was taken back to England. There it was drawn and its portrait published as 'a blue-bellied parrot'.

The next landfall was made at Bustard Bay and it was in search of fresh water rather than specimens. Another brief landing for scarce water was made at Thirsty Sound on 29 May where ants' nests 'made of clay, as big as a bushel' were found on the branches of trees, and there was a dramatic encounter with a cloud of amazing black and blue butterflies. 'The air was for a space of 3 or 4 acres crowded with them to a wonderful degree. The eye could not be turned in any direction without seeing millions and every branch and twig was almost covered with those that sat

Kangaroo *Macropus* sp.
**By Sydney Parkinson.
Kangaroos were first seen
by the crew of the *Endeavour*
at Endeavour River.**
BM(NH)

still.' Banks's entry in his journal captures the mood of wonderful delight at this exotic experience.

Denied much opportunity to explore the land, the party was just as active at sea. The water was trawled with nets for marine plankton and fishing went on continually, though after the catch was carefully examined and recorded it was handed over to the cook. One more landfall was made at Green Island, just beyond the Whitsunday Passage, the day before the near-wreck of the *Endeavour*. The next few days drew everyone's mind back to simple survival, though Banks was aware that many of their specimens would be lost when the bread compartment where they had been stored was flooded.

It was not until the damaged ship had been successfully beached and a camp made at the mouth of the Endeavour River that Banks's party was able to make their most thorough examination of the Australian environment. Cook had been unable to allow as much time at anchor as Banks would have liked and this time he was not to be deterred from exploration, even by the mosquitoes that devoured them all. Banks organized a 3-day boat trip up the Endeavour River. Two hundred more plant species were gathered, of which Parkinson made 190 preliminary sketches. Numerous birds were recorded and Parkinson made a drawing of a red-tailed black cockatoo that was the only one he would complete of an Australian bird.

It was at Endeavour Bay that several sightings were made. For the first time a kangaroo was sighted. From the few fleeting glimpses it seemed to be about as large as a greyhound, mouse-coloured and too swift for the dogs. When finally one was shot Banks recorded that 'to compare it to any European animal would be impossible . . .' The kangaroo was given to the cook, but not before Parkinson had made two pencil sketches. Banks brought the skull and the skin back to England, and a description and illustration was published in the official account of the voyage in 1773.

As well as the kangaroo, a small number of animals were collected and others sighted in the closely timbered country. In the circumstances there were no doubt many other imaginative rather than accurate descriptions, such as the one by a sailor of a creature as large as a gallon keg and 'as black as the Devil' with two horns on its head, assumed to have been inspired by a fruit bat.

Parkinson listed uncertainly 'goats, wolves, a small red animal about the size of a squirrel' and 'a spotted one of the vivera kind'. In the bush Banks found a female opossum with two young. 'This creature' noted Parkinson, 'has a membraneous bag near the stomach in which it conceals and carries its young when it is apprehensive of danger.'

Preserving animal specimens for any length of time was a much more difficult problem than preserving plant specimens. Small animals could be preserved in glass, stoppered bottles filled with rum brought for this purpose from England. They took up scarce space, needing to be stored in strong cases. To store larger animals whole kegs of rum were necessary and rum itself must have been an increasingly scarce commodity at this extreme point of the *Endeavour's* voyage. However, even botanical specimens presented problems for preservation and storage, and so a great deal of effort went into collecting seeds. A store of different sorts of salts was carried in the *Endeavour* for the then approved method of securing seeds from which plants could be germinated later. Seeds were bedded in sand in a corked cylindrical glass bottle which was then suspended in a larger bottle and the space between filled with a mixture of nitre, common salt and sal ammoniac. Banks was always experimenting, hoping to find the best methods to make sure that valuable specimens would survive the extreme conditions faced on a long sea voyage.

It was easier to assemble a compact collection of butterflies, beetles, ants, moths, mantids and flies from the thriving insect life found everywhere. Shells were picked up by everyone including the ship's officers and crew. They offered no problem of storage or preservation and were sure to

Green turtle
Chelonia mydas,
sketched by Sydney Parkinson at Endeavour River.
BM(NH)

find buyers among private collectors in England. Cook and Banks had their own personal collection and Solander, who catalogued Banks's collection, later catalogued one for the Duchess of Portland, regarded as one of the finest in Europe, that included such specimens as the Sydney rock oyster.

On the return of the *Endeavour* to England, Banks and Solander found themselves instant celebrities, and early scientific queries had to wait. 'They are so busy getting their things on shore and seeing their friends that they have scarce time to tell us of anything but the many narrow escapes they have had from imminent danger', wrote one impatient acquaintance. Banks and Solander had good reason to be aware of these realities. Though Banks returned full of his customary energy and vitality, apparently unharmed by his brush with fever at Batavia, where he and Solander had been nursed back to health on land, Solander had been 'a great deal indisposed'. The homecoming must have brought back to them forcibly the personal cost of the voyage. Of Banks's party of eight only half had survived, he and Solander and his Lincolnshire assistants. Young Buchan had been buried at Tahiti and Parkinson and Spöring had been buried at sea.

In a social and scientific round Banks was presented at Court, beginning a long association with King George III. Solander and Banks were awarded honorary degrees by the University of Oxford, and Banks found himself a member of the scientific elite that composed the Royal Society Club. Replacing Spöring, Solander became Banks's secretary and librarian and went to live with him at his London house 'amid the books, herbarium specimens and natural curiosities in his care'.

In spite of the great collection Banks managed to bring back to England there was not to be a great deal of information published about it at first. The official account of the voyage, published in 1773, as well as several other unofficial accounts published about the same time, prepared the way for the first public interest in the amazing plants and animals of the new continent. Some early information circulated in the scientific community by word of mouth and especially through the membership of the Royal Society and through contact with Banks himself. Banks had kept a meticulous journal, but no arrangements were made for its publication until a century later when Sir Joseph Hooker edited and published, in a very abbreviated form, the *Journal of Sir Joseph Banks*. Solander also published little. After the abandonment of Banks's intention to join Cook's second voyage, the arrangement and classification of the great collection already made was postponed for further expeditions made by Banks and Solander to Scotland, Wales and Ireland. In the year that the official account of the voyage was released Solander was appointed Keeper of the natural history collection at the British Museum. He gave his name to a book-box for carrying notes and specimens, and to several plant species.

Nevertheless it was an age of eager speculative curiosity that convinced men like the American Thomas Jefferson, when he pocketed some rice seeds from Piedmont in Italy, that the greatest service that could be rendered any nation was to add a useful plant to its stock. Participation in Cook's first voyage had an immense effect on Banks. There were many who agreed with Linnaeus, who wrote, 'I cannot sufficiently admire Mr Banks who has exposed himself to so many dangers and has bestowed more money in the service of Natural Science than any other man. Surely none but an Englishman would have the spirit to do what he has done.'

Banks was to continue to devote much of his life and his considerable fortune to the patronage of science. The pattern he had set of attaching naturalists to voyages of exploration was widely followed and gave opportunity for travel to many famous naturalists. In 1778 Banks was elected President of the Royal Society and controlled its affairs for the next 42 years. He was to become the organizer and co-ordinator of projects for the advancement of scientific research, especially anything of practical use. His house at 32 Soho Square, London, became an international centre for discussion and exchange of information. His herbarium, unrivalled collections and library were available to all who could profit by their use.

After his celebrated voyage with Cook, Banks's authority on the remote Southern Ocean and its lands was never questioned. His own interest in the region was permanent, and he was to play a leading role in the colonization and development of Australia.

32 Soho Square

Banksia, *Banksia serrata*,
detail of engraved copper plate by J F Miller.
BM(NH)

Banks's florilegium

Sydney Parkinson was the first professional artist to set foot in Australia and it was chiefly through the published engravings of his work, made by other artists, that the new continent made its first impact on Europe. Many of the engravings were produced as illustrations for the journals and accounts of the voyage of the *Endeavour* that were the only public sources of information of the time. Banks was able to make sure that only the most skilled engravers were employed for the publication of these results, and by his own supervision tried to ensure that the translation from Parkinson's original work was as accurate as possible.

However the botanical impact of the *Endeavour*'s voyage was as great as the geographical one. Banks had returned to England with a treasure store of plant specimens and descriptions of exotic flora. The scientific community of Europe waited, fascinated, for further news of what an excited Linnaeus called a 'matchless and truly astonishing collection such as has never been seen before, nor may ever be seen again'. Some 1300 new species and 110 new genera were determined from it. After the return to England Solander laboured to complete a descriptive botanical catalogue which needed only the appropriate illustrations before it was published.

Banksia, *Banksia serrata*, original specimen from Botany Bay. Drawn by Parkinson and described by Solander.
BM(NH)

Banksia, *Banksia serrata*, original sketch and colour key drawing by Sydney Parkinson. Drawn at Botany Bay from the fresh specimen.
BM(NH)

From an early stage it had been Banks's intention to publish an ambitious botanical work, a 'florilegium', literally, a gathering of flowers. This would have been the most effective way to make accurate information available to botanists. This great project was to be based on engravings of the priceless drawings of plants made by Sydney Parkinson during the voyage.

Such was Parkinson's developed skill and comprehensive eye that he had managed to produce a staggering 955 botanical drawings. These were the original pencil sketches he had made of each specimen as they were given to him. His first concern was always to capture the true colours of the plants before they dried and faded. In order to deal quickly with the plants that poured in, Parkinson would paint in detail a single leaf and flower, or seedhead. Then he would make detailed notes on the reverse with careful colour guides so that he could finish the work at a later stage. He would return to his sketches in the long periods at sea and work them up into completed watercolour paintings. He had completed only 269 of these before his death at sea.

After the return of the expedition Banks paid Parkinson's sister and brother £500 for Sydney's drawings and papers as well as his collection of curios. This amount also included the balance of his salary. Banks

Banksia, *Banksia serrata*, watercolour based on the Parkinson sketch. Drawn in England by J F Miller under Banks's instruction.
BM(NH)

Banksia, *Banksia serrata*, final hand-finished print (1986) from the engravings initially commissioned by Banks for his florilegium.
BM(NH)

then employed artists to complete Parkinson's works from all this material combined with the actual specimens, now pressed and dried. Banks had expected to accompany Cook on his second voyage, and had hardly returned home before he set about making lavish new preparations for 'this, my favourite undertaking'. He had already collected a team of 12 and begun elaborate alterations to the structure of Cook's ship the *Resolution* before the Admiralty stepped in and restrained these plans so strictly that Banks withdrew his scientific and artistic suite from the expedition. After this disappointment his chosen artists Frederick Nodder, John and James Miller and John Cleveley were diverted to make watercolour paintings from Parkinson's unfinished sketches. Banks made himself available to give advice and guidance to the artists as the work progressed, though the process was less methodical than it sounded because Banks developed many other interests.

Nevertheless, in 1780 Banks began to employ a team of engravers who after 7 years had finished 550 copper plates. This was only about half the work. After 13 years the comparative pace of production had slowed down considerably. Only 743 engraved copper plates were ready. Banks had invested many thousands of pounds in this project, but as the years went by the florilegium clearly lost its impetus, and in the end was never completed.

There were a number of possible reasons for the failure to publish the results of such industry and the most likely explanation was the steady complication and development of Banks's personal responsibilities over these years. In addition, Solander who shared in a great deal of this knowledge and on whom Banks depended heavily as librarian and secretary, died in 1782. But the consequences of a dispute with Parkinson's brother, Stanfield, might have been expected to affect the project. Banks had lent Sydney's papers and drawings to Stanfield after he had purchased them from the family. Contrary to Banks's stipulation, Stanfield had them copied for publication. Banks had obtained a legal injunction preventing this publication until

the official account of the voyage of the *Endeavour* had appeared in 1773. It is perhaps because of this dispute that John Hawkesworth, the official editor of the published account of the voyage, made no acknowledgement of Parkinson's work. Though his papers were used his name did not appear on the plates taken from his drawings, only two of which were of Australian subjects.

Though to the disappointment of many publication of Banks's florilegium did not proceed, the engraved copper plates and the completed drawings, along with the notes and original specimens, were freely available for study at Banks's home. The plates and paintings and his herbarium were bequeathed to the British Museum (Natural History) after his death in 1820. The work of those early artists and engravers was published for the first time when in 1900-05 the Museum issued 318 black-and-white lithographs made from the copper plates, with their descriptions by Solander, as *Illustrations of Australian Plants collected in 1770 during Captain Cook's voyage round the World in H.M.S. Endeavour* (edited by James Britten). To celebrate Captain Cook's bicentenary in 1973 another issue was made, limited to 100 prints. During 1979-88 the exacting task of producing 100 copies of the entire set of the 738 original florilegium copper plates in colour was undertaken. After 200 years Banks's vision has been realized and Parkinson's craftmanship revealed.

A young man 'of singular simplicity of conduct', the youthful Parkinson had won respect for his skill even before the departure of the *Endeavour*. Born in Edinburgh, the son of a brewer and a Quaker, gentle and conscientious, but no less determined, Parkinson's natural attraction to botanical drawing had taken him to London. His delicate artistry could already be appreciated in the paintings of flowers on silk he exhibited with the Royal Society of Arts. He found employment in London making drawings for James Lee, the prominent Hammersmith nurseryman.

Parkinson was employed by Banks to make watercolour drawings of mammals and birds brought from Sri Lanka. (These drawings are now in the possession of the

British Museum (Natural History).) He also worked on the collection Banks had brought back from his expedition to Newfoundland and Labrador. When offered the opportunity to join the *Endeavour* as botanical draughtsman at an annual salary of £80 'an insatiable curiosity for such researches prevailed over every other consideration', according to his brother. The hazards of the voyage were not lost on Parkinson, however, and before he left he made his will in favour of his sister Brittania.

During the voyage of the *Endeavour* Parkinson had turned his hand to other than botanical subjects. Altogether he produced some 1300 drawings, about two-thirds of which were sketches rather than finished drawings. Fortunately a great quantity of Parkinson's work has survived. Of 18 volumes of his plant drawings held by the British Museum there are eight volumes (243 drawings) of Australian plants. There are also three volumes of zoological subjects including some sketches relating to Australia. Besides his now well-known plant and animal drawings, Parkinson was the first to attempt sketches of the Australian landscape and to draw aboriginals from direct observations. In 1773 his brother used his papers to publish *A Journal of a Voyage to the South Seas,* and a second edition, enlarged, followed in 1784. The book was illustrated with Parkinson's drawings, including the first known portrait of an Australian aboriginal.

Though he had great skill as a natural history draughtsman, Parkinson was too young and independent not to be interested in all aspects of the great adventure he was involved in. He was only 2 years younger than Banks and shared his same candid scientific curiosity, so that he took time to attempt to compile vocabularies of the languages he heard in Tahiti and in New Holland. Perhaps because of his disciplined artist's eye he was an unusually balanced and accurate observer and the natural straightforward style of his writing is as vivid in its effect as is his drawing.

Barringtonia calyptrata.
By Sydney Parkinson,
completed by F P Nodder.

The First Fleet at Rio de Janeiro, Brazil.
By George Raper. The only contemporary
picture of the complete fleet.
BM(NH)

Chapter 5

First Fleet 1770–1788

In 1776, the year that James Cook set out on his third and last voyage of exploration, a long and damaging war broke out between Britain and her American colonies. As the war spread France and Spain became involved, and peace was not achieved with all parties until 1784. The end of the American War of Independence brought fresh problems to Britain. After the war the time-honoured system of sending convicted criminals to America ended when the newly independent colonies abolished the system. Post-war conditions in Britain led to prisons being so overcrowded that convicts were crammed into rotting old ship hulks.

Even before the end of the war a House of Commons Committee (1779) had considered the advantages of continuing the system of transportation. As part of their deliberations they listened to evidence about other places to which convicts might profitably be sent. Joseph Banks appeared before the Committee and confidently recommended New Holland and specifically Botany Bay as his preference for a new British settlement. Apart from his belief that the east coast of Australia could support a sizeable population, Banks obviously thought that there was certain to be something of value in such a vast tract of land. Cook's return from his third voyage was expected to end all speculation about this region, but his tragic death at Tahiti in 1779 left the question unsettled.

It was not until after the end of the American War of Independence that the British government, faced with many post-war crises, returned to the unsolved problem of whether to renew the old system of transportation. After some hesitation it committed itself to the colonization of a still barely-known Australia. In August 1786 Botany Bay on the east coast of Australia was decided on as the site for a British colony.

Grave political problems added weight to the choice of Australia. Britain had lost her American colonies, and with them important resources and an export market. It was believed that war was brewing again with Spain and France and with this threat came the danger of being unable to defend vital trade routes to India and China.

Under all these pressures, a permanent British settlement in Australia seemed to offer attractive advantages. It could solve the political problem of overcrowded gaols, in the event of war it would give safe anchorage to shipping, and eventually the untapped continent must open up new trade routes and markets.

Preparations were hurriedly begun. A fleet of 11 ships was got ready and a search was made for a 'discreet officer' to command it. The choice of a naval officer, Arthur Phillip (1738-1814) as captain of the *Sirius* and Governor-Elect of New South Wales was announced by Lord Sydney, the Secretary of State for the Home Department. Phillip was then 48 years old, a small active man with an aquiline nose and a sharp and powerful voice. A post-captain in command of a 64 gun ship at the end of the American war, Phillip had been on half-pay since May 1784.

The crisis in the penal system in the 1770's led to the overspill of convicts being housed in rotting ship hulks.

An experienced career officer, he had been in all the major engagements fought by the British Navy since he had joined it as a humble 'captain's servant' at the age of 17.

Phillip took up this novel responsibility with energy and enthusiasm. Until the very last moment he was occupied in examining proposals and plans for the colony he must establish which would be 6 months' voyage from the nearest aid, and 18 months from England across hazardous and barely navigated ocean. No detail was too small for his attention and only his industry and forethought, exercised before the First Fleet left England, prevented a disaster.

Most of Phillip's problems were practical ones arising from the uncertainties of pioneering: how much food to take and how to preserve it; what was needed to begin agriculture and horticulture; how to regulate the convicts and military garrison that travelled with them; what port orders to issue for the Fleet. Phillip showed

Arthur Phillip (1738–1814), commander of the First Fleet and first Governor of New South Wales. By Francis Wheatley, oil on canvas. NPG

advanced and humanitarian views. In considering the future of his colony, he had a more glorious object in mind than a mere penal settlement, for he wrote in an early memorandum, 'I would not wish convicts to lay the foundation of an Empire', and he was concerned that the colony should be considered in this way from the beginning, for he also emphasized that 'there can be no slavery in a free land, and consequently no slaves'.

On a signal given at daylight from Phillip's ship, the whole fleet was under sail before 6 a.m. on 13 May 1787. The expedition, now known as the First Fleet, of two Admiralty vessels (a frigate *Sirius* and an armed tender, the *Supply*) accompanied by six convict transports and three storeships, sailed from Portsmouth. Altogether there were 1450 people on board, of whom about half were men and women sentenced to transportation. The long voyage was fairly free of incident or disaster. It touched first at Tenerife (Canary Islands) and next at Rio de Janeiro where Phillip was very courteously received by the Portuguese Viceroy of the Brazils. His respect for Phillip, who spoke Portuguese fluently, was largely due to

Phillip's reputation for courage and skill acquired while serving with the Portuguese navy for several years.

Phillip had intended to replenish and load his major stores at Cape Town, but when the fleet arrived at the Dutch Cape of Good Hope, there was general scarcity. The Dutch governor gave permission to purchase these necessities extremely reluctantly, and in part only, despite hard bargaining by Phillip. As the Fleet left the Cape, anxiety about the last stage of the journey mingled in the minds of those on board with regret at the thought of leaving behind 'every scene of civilization and humanized manners to explore a remote and barbarous land'.

Soon after leaving the Cape, Phillip decided to split the Fleet. He separated the four fastest sailing ships, including the *Supply,* in which he travelled, intending to get to Botany Bay in time to choose the best site for the settlement and begin preparations to receive those following in the slower ships. He therefore transferred to the faster ships all the sawyers, carpenters, blacksmiths and other useful men to begin building at Botany Bay.

On 18 January 1788 a small wooden

The First Fleet, with Table Mountain, Cape Town in the background. By George Raper. BM(NH)

sailing ship nosed into Botany Bay on the deserted shore of New South Wales. It was the *Supply,* 20 hours ahead of the three other ships. Unfortunately, Phillip's careful plan did not succeed, for in 3 days all the ships of the Fleet had anchored in the bay. It was over 8 months since they had sailed from England, and 3 months since they had left the Cape of Good Hope. Everyone gazed curiously at the grey-green wilderness that faced them, but even isolation was momentarily forgotten in the prospect of setting foot on land again. One new arrival paused long enough to note that

... the spirits visible in every eye was to be ascribed to the general joy and satisfaction which immediately took place

on finding ourselves arrived at that port which had been so much and so long the subject of our most serious reflections, the constant theme of our conversations.

In this interval Phillip had been struck by the disadvantages of Botany Bay, an exposed harbour with hidden shallows, and its waterless interior. He set off north on 21 January to explore and on 23 January ordered the Fleet to leave for Sydney Cove within neighbouring Port Jackson 'the finest harbour in the world'. He had several good reasons for this change of plan. He was delighted with the advantages of the great inner harbour where, he wrote, 'a thousand ship of the line could ride in perfect safety'. Sydney Cove itself was supplied with an essential spring of

fresh water and ships could anchor there so close to the shore that wharfs could be constructed quickly and cheaply at which the largest of ships could unload.

Landing operations began when Phillip founded Sydney, named after the Secretary of State, on 26 January 1788. Most of the convicts who had been on board the transport ships for nearly 12 months were not landed until some preparations were made on land to receive them. Some advance gangs felled trees and cleared the thick bush on both sides of the spring, known as the Tank Stream. Others set up a blacksmith's forge, unloaded stores or set up tents and marquees. The marines, glad to re-establish land discipline, exercised and paraded, while

The First Fleet reached Port Jackson after an 8 month voyage from Portsmouth.

cooks stoked up blazing fires to prepare food.

In one of the first published accounts of the colony, *A Narrative of the Expedition to Botany Bay* (London 1789), Watkin Tench, an officer of marines with the Fleet, described that early scene,

Into the head of the cove, on which our establishment is fixed, runs a small stream of freshwater, which serves to divide the adjacent country to a little distance, in the direction of north and south. On the eastern side of this rivulet the Governor fixed his place of residence, with a large body of convicts encamped near him; and on the western side was disposed the remaining part of these people, near the marine encampment.

Phillip himself had brought a prefabricated canvas house, the marines had tents and the convicts shared some dockyard canvas. There was not enough to go round so they built shelters of anything they could use, especially the cabbage tree palms that then grew around Sydney Cove.

On 7 February the convicts were assembled, and the red-coated marines drawn up with their colours flying and band playing. Under the brilliant blue sky, and surrounded by the heavy silence of the bush, the company listened while the commission was read that defined the Governor's powers in the new colony. Phillip then made a 'pointed and judicious' speech assuring the convicts of his interest in their welfare, and urging good

behaviour and co-operation which he promised would be rewarded by clemency. Then, having reviewed the ranks of marines, he invited the officers to dine with him.

Several days before this ceremony Phillip had sent a party of convicts and marines to establish a second settlement at Norfolk Island. The decision was carried out quickly after the sudden, unexpected appearance of two ships of a French expedition of discovery. The Admiralty, however, had been interested from the outset in Norfolk Island, hoping that sailcloth and cordage might be manufactured from the flax Cook had reported growing there on his second voyage (1774). There was also great

The settlement at Port Jackson. By George Raper. BM(NH)

interest in the distinctive pine trees on the island which it was hoped would provide timber for ships' masts. On the outward voyage in the *Sirius,* Lieutenant Henry Ball discovered and named Lord Howe Island. Norfolk Island proved to have rich, fertile soil excellent for cultivation. Phillip, increasingly desperate as months dragged by without the arrival of ships from England with further supplies, ferried more and more troops and convicts to the island until it supported nearly one-third of the people who had landed at Sydney.

The first few months at Sydney were filled with disappointments. In spite of the preparations made before the Fleet left, many necessities, including convict record papers and the women convicts' clothing had been left behind. Clothing which was generally scarce and never very hard-wearing was soon tattered, and even the marines were eventually seen standing guard without shoes. The food stores turned out to be 'poor in quality, short in quantity or missing'. As everyone was dependent on these stores for their very existence until the next ships arrived from England, all food issued was strictly rationed.

Short rations weakened the convicts so that their hours of labour had to be cut. The first concern had been to provide shelter and security for the public stores, so temporary wooden storehouses were built. Heavy summer rain and the advance of the first winter encouraged efforts to make the Sydney Cove settlement more permanent. A hospital was the next priority, and then small two-roomed huts of wattle and daub with thatched roofs were put up for married couples. The marines were eager to escape from their tents. As Watkin Tench explained,

A transient view of those gay camps, near the metropolis, which so many remember, naturally draws forth careless and unmeaning exclamations of rapture, which attach ideas of pleasure only, to this part of a soldier's life. But an encampment amidst the rocks and wilds of a new country, aggravated by the miseries of a bad diet, and incessant toil, will find few admirers.

To the dismay of the marines, the shortage of labour meant that they had to build their own barracks. The convicts were all sheltered before the onset of winter, but the soldiers remained in their

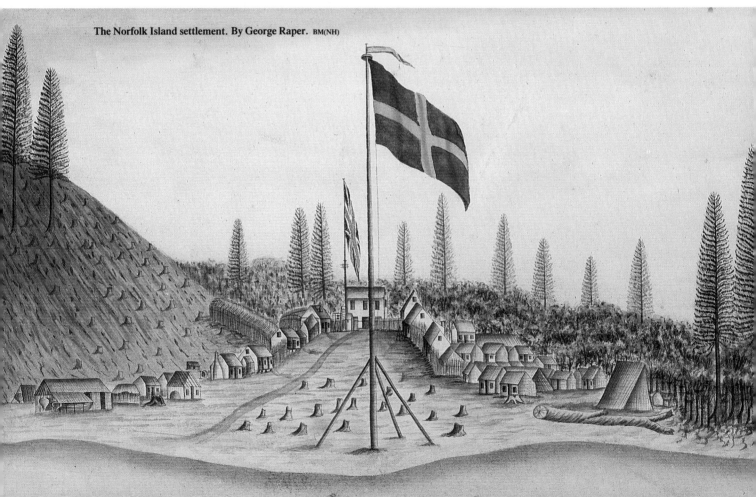

The Norfolk Island settlement. By George Raper. BM(NH)

tents which were covered with bushes as insulation against the cold.

The decision made about the location of the first settlement at Sydney was of major importance to the beginning of land exploration in Australia. All around Port Jackson there was thick scrub and little sign of fresh water, and Phillip grew increasingly anxious to penetrate this wilderness. Despite his numerous responsibilities he himself explored the surrounding coastal waterways and forests, to search for land suitable for cultivation and further settlement.

Only 6 weeks after the first landing he went with two small boats to examine a neighbouring area described by Cook as 'broken land'. On 2 March 1788 he entered an inlet, thinking it was Cook's Broken Bay and discovered another fine stretch of water that he described as being 'of sufficient extent to contain all the navy of Great Britain'. After spending the night there in the boat, to avoid being surprised by the numerous aboriginals seen on the shores, Phillip named it Pitt Water, after England's prime minister, William Pitt.

His first expedition into the surrounding country showed how difficult it was going to be to travel in the bush. Phillip's aim was to try to reach a chain of mountains which could be seen in clear weather from some hills near the settlement, for he was convinced that the 'Blue Mountains' must be the source of a great river. With a party of 11 Phillip set off by water to Manly Cove, where the party left their boats and went north-west on foot. After 4 days of struggling through the thickly wooded country, their provisions began to run out and they turned back while still 20 miles from the base of the mountains. Several months later Phillip took another party to examine the coastline between Manly Cove and Broken Bay. It was not until mid-1789 than an important discovery was made of the outlet of a freshwater river which Phillip named the 'Hawkesbury'. For many years it was to be easier to move about the area by boat, and Phillip organized an expedition by water to try and trace the source of the Hawkesbury which was to play an important part in the history of the colony. The expedition

traced the windings of the river northwards for over 60 miles before they were blocked by a waterfall.

Early attempts at agriculture were depressing. The first land cleared was not particularly fertile, and was very difficult to prepare, partly because it was baked dry and stump-ridden, but also because few good tools had been sent with the Fleet. 'I beg leave to observe that bad tools are of no kind of use', Phillip wrote with feeling in one of his despatches to the Home Office. Few of the convicts actually knew anything about agriculture, and their experience in England was not very useful in this new land, where the seasons were reversed. The seed that had been brought to sow did not adapt to the different conditions, and much of it had germinated on the voyage out, making it useless for planting.

The near-failure of the first crops brought home to the colony the stern prospect of starvation. Within 6 months of landing 'fresh provisions were become scarcer than in a blockaded town', and as a result of the absence of fresh food, scurvy began to make its appearance. A small store of livestock brought with the Fleet for

breeding and stocking the colony was not to be killed for food but a major disaster occurred when all the cattle escaped from their convict keeper and disappeared into the bush. During the early months of settlement plentiful supplies of fishes had been caught in the harbour but unaccountably, when they were most needed, they became so scarce that an officer wrote that they were 'rarely seen at the tables of the first among us'. Stray kangaroos, birds, and even snakes, became delicacies, available only to those with guns.

Pressed hard by the need to ensure food for the future, Phillip set up a third settlement before the end of 1788, at Rose Hill, about 15 miles inland, and west of Sydney. Good agricultural soil had been found in this area and some convicts and marines were sent to set up a government farm and begin another settlement there. Later, known by the aboriginal name Parramatta, it was to become a flourishing centre. A fortnight after the establishment of Rose Hill the last convict transports sailed, leaving only the *Supply* in Sydney Cove. The departure of these large whaling ships, whose mere presence had been

The Government farm at Rose Hill. Unknown artist. BM(NH)

comforting, left an acute sense of desolation in the colony which was already uneasy that no news had come from England. The growing sense of abandonment was heightened by Phillip's unavoidable decision to send the *Sirius* to the Cape of Good Hope for provisions. The *Sirius* did not return for over 7 months, having circumnavigated the world on her journey by way of New Zealand and Cape Horn.

The provisions the *Sirius* brought helped Phillip to avoid having to further reduce rations until early in 1790. As no ships had come from England by then he sent the *Sirius* to China for further supplies. On 5 April, seeing the signal for the approach of a ship, the Governor went excitedly down

to the harbour only to be told of the wreck of the *Sirius* off Norfolk Island. The colony's situation was now desperate and Phillip called together all the civil and military officers to discuss the position. Rations were again reduced, this time to 2 pounds of salted pork, 2½ pounds of rice and a quart of pease a week for all adults. Their only ship and last lifeline, the *Supply,* was sent to Batavia for provisions while the sea was combed for fishes, and the best marksmen were sent off into the bush for game to supplement the rations. Food was so scarce that even those invited to dine with the Governor had to bring their own bread.

Some of the earliest surviving pictorial records of these days were made by

George Raper (1768?-1797), a midshipman with the First Fleet. Raper, like Phillip, entered the navy (1783) as a captain's servant and joined the *Sirius* as an able seaman, though he had been promoted to midshipman before the end of the voyage. Raper was no professional artist, but he had the ability to make a graphic record vivid in its simplicity. During the voyage he made watercolour drawings of events associated with the First Fleet, then of the foundation of the colony and also of the settlement at Norfolk Island. He also made many of the first natural history paintings of the birds and flowers of Sydney Cove. As an added embellishment to many of his paintings of birds, Raper added careful and accurate drawings of flowers or insects.

HMS *Sirius*,
wrecked at Norfolk Island
while delivering provisions.
By George Raper.
BM(NH)

Lord Howe Island Pigeon
Janthaenas godmanae.

Eastern grey kangaroo
Macropus giganteus.
Grass tree
Xanthorrhoea sp.

Red-tailed tropic bird
Phaethon rubricauda.

Emu
Dromaius novaehollandiae.

51

The British Museum (Natural History) holds a volume of 73 drawings signed by Raper of scenes, native implements, birds, flowers, fishes and other subjects.

Very much part of the colony's pioneering, Raper went with the *Sirius* to the Cape of Good Hope when it was sent for supplies. When the *Sirius* was wrecked at Norfolk Island Raper was marooned there with his shipmates for almost a year. He put his stay to good use making watercolours of the wreck of the *Sirius,* of the settlement and of some of the island's birdlife. Many of his drawings are still valuable to ornithologists as the only illustrations of now extinct bird species, such as the Lord Howe Island pigeon. Little is known of his life after he returned to England in the Dutch ship *Waaksamheyd* hired to replace the *Sirius*. He was paid off some weeks after his arrival in April 1792, but was then promoted to lieutenant in June and served in the *Cumberland.* On his death only a few weeks later in 1797 Raper was described as the 'Late Commander of HMS *Cutter* expedition'. His will, which has survived, bequeathed his drawings to his relatives and provided that 'All other things, Drawing Papers and Books excepted, I desire may be sold at the Mast as is the Custom at Sea.'

The sheer struggle for existence absorbed most of the community's available labour but ground was surveyed and marked out for Sydney's main buildings. From the beginning Phillip had had radical and far-sighted ideas about the town he intended to create. It was to be a spacious city, because as Watkin Tench agreed, 'extent of empire demands grandeur of design'. The principal street

View of Port Jackson showing the Governor's house. Unknown artist. BM(NH)

was to be 200 feet wide with other streets in corresponding proportions. There were to be no crowded rows of mean buildings which encouraged slums, for all buildings were to have adequate land to prevent overcrowding and pestilence. Land within the town was to remain the property of the Crown and was only to be leased.

When good clay was discovered an advance was quickly made towards permanence. A kiln was built and bricklaying began. All houses had to be restricted to one storey until lime was available to make mortar, but the Governor's house was an exception. It had a second storey and lime for this building was laboriously manufactured by burning shells. At first the only two solid dwellings in the settlement were those of the Governor and the Lieutenant-Governor, though an abundance of fine sandstone allowed masons to begin building permanent houses for officials.

The King's birthday was celebrated on 4 June 1789 by a dinner in the newly completed Governor's house, followed by a public performance of the popular contemporary play 'The Recruiting Officer'.

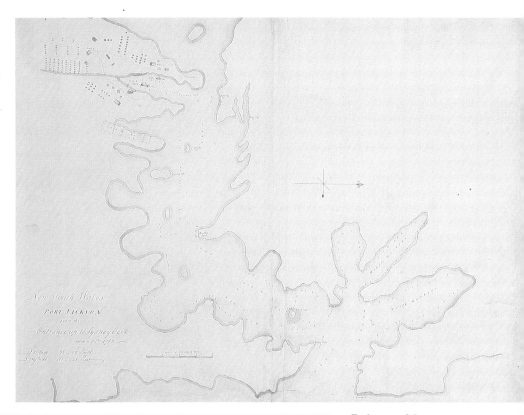

Early map of the area around Port Jackson. By Thomas Watling.
BM(NH)

Brickfield hill where clay for brick production was first located. Engraving from Collins' *Account of the English colony in New South Wales.*

53

The settlement at Port Jackson.
By Thomas Watling.
BM(NH)

Chapter 6
First settlement 1790–1820

It was 2 years after the arrival of the First Fleet at Sydney Cove before another ship from England appeared. The *Lady Juliana* arrived in June 1790 carrying women convicts. She was the first ship of the 'Second Fleet' to reach New South Wales. The *Lady Juliana* also brought news – the colony learned for the first time of the outbreak of the French Revolution. Although she brought more mouths to feed, the settlement was delirious with delight. The fearful suspicion of having been forgotten or abandoned was wiped out when it was learned that a store ship, the *Guardian,* intended to reach Sydney months before, had been wrecked near Cape Town. A few days later the *Justinian* arrived, loaded entirely with stores, so that full rations could be restored.

Within the month five ships arrived, bringing nearly 1000 convicts. Unlike the much healthier First Fleet, many had died on the passage, and a great number were sickly. But there were now more labourers, tools and seed. Superintendents for the convicts had been included for the first time too, so that their labour was to be more effective. The Second Fleet brought new purpose to the colony. Philip wrote, 'I hope after all our disappointments that two years more will fix this Colony beyond the reach of accidents; . . . if it fails I shall fail with it . . . but of which I really have no apprehensions.'

Immediately he planned new buildings and ordered more ground to be cleared at Rose Hill. More and more convicts were transferred to Rose Hill where Phillip had another residence built which he visited often. Cultivation was given up at Sydney, where the crops had almost totally failed. At first there was still not enough food and Phillip issued plots of ground to any convicts whose sentence had expired, and who volunteered to become settlers. He would have been quite happy 'to have all the Convicts changed into fifty good farmers'.

The constant menace of starvation was not the only problem that occupied the Governor. Before his arrival the native inhabitants still were an unknown quantity. As Parkinson had written of Cook's attempts to make contact, 'The natives

The settlement at Port Jackson. By Thomas Watling. BM(NH)

Surgeon John White and others talking with aboriginals. Unknown artist. BM(NH)

often reconnoitred us, but we could not prevail on them to come near us to to be social'. Phillip's official instructions urged him to be friendly if possible, and to send back to England all the information of scientific interest about the aboriginals that he might be able to gather. As was his practice, Phillip had already thought the matter out. His chief concern was to maintain peace with justice. While he was prepared for a hostile reception, he did not intend to let violence reign. In his very first despatch from Sydney he wrote,

With respect to the natives, it was my determination, from my first landing that nothing less than the most absolute necessity should ever make me fire upon them, and tho' persevering in this resolution has at times been rather difficult I have hitherto been so fortunate that it has never been necessary.

When the First Fleet arrived the aboriginals were found to be much more numerous than Captain Cook's reports had given reason to expect. Both races were curious about one another and cautious as well. The main problem was how to establish communication, and it was decided reluctantly that the only way was to capture an aboriginal and teach him some English, in the hope that he would then act as an interpreter. At Manly Cove an aboriginal named Arabanoo was taken captive. Arabanoo, who was about 30 years old, was taken into the Governor's household, given clothing and introduced to the strangers' food and manners. However, when Phillip took him back to Manly Cove to talk with his own people, they would have nothing to do with him. Arabanoo's capture, therefore, did little to create understanding, and incidents between the two groups became more frequent and worrying.

Phillip took precautions to prevent aboriginals being exposed to insult or interference, intending that when there was an opportunity to mix with them, they should be encouraged to live among the settlers, and be taught the advantages of cultivating the land. Being concerned to deal fairly, he always carefully examined all accounts of hostile encounters brought by the convicts. When 16 convicts, who attacked the aboriginals to steal their fishing tackle and spears, were routed and seven of them were wounded and one killed, Phillip sent marines out to quell the trouble and had the offending convicts flogged in front of the aboriginals.

In April 1789 an epidemic of smallpox killed many aboriginals, including Arabanoo, whose demise caused great concern amongst the settlers, with whom he had become popular. Phillip decided to try again, and had two more natives (Benelong and Colbee) brought into the settlement. Colbee was an accomplished warrior who escaped within a week. Benelong, however, seemed to accept his captivity, and his huge appetite taxed the resources of the hungry settlement for the few weeks before he, too, escaped.

When, in September 1790, Phillip learned that Benelong and Colbee had

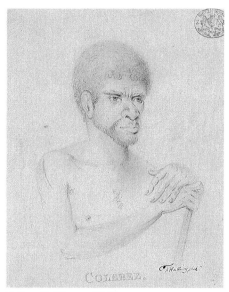

Colbee. By Thomas Watling. BM(NH)

Benelong. Unknown artist. BM(NH)

Aboriginals chasing rush cutters. Unknown artist. BM(NH)

been seen with other aboriginals at Manly Cove he immediately went to meet them there. While he was trying to talk with them another aboriginal speared Phillip through the shoulder. After a painful journey back to Sydney by boat his wound was found to be not as serious as had been feared. It healed quickly and he refused to take reprisals as he believed the aboriginal had not actually been hostile.

A few months later the Governor's convict gamekeeper was killed when he approached some aboriginals unarmed. Seventeen people had already been killed in isolated attacks, but previously Phillip had not been sure if this was the result of provocation or misunderstanding. This time he felt he had to make an example, or unprovoked killings would endanger the settlement. He ordered out a large search party to bring in six aboriginals, but the party failed to find any. When a second expedition was sent with the same result, the subject of punishment was dropped. Henceforth, relations between the first colonists and the aboriginals were neither clearly harmonious nor hostile and varied according to the motives of either side.

Within the settlement the civil officers continued to pursue their scientific curiousity and the convicts to grumble about what they saw as unfair indulgence towards the aboriginals. 'They are treated with the most singular tenderness' wrote one convict. He was able to concede, however,

That the inhabitants of N.S. Wales are centuries behind some other savage nations, in point of useful knowledge, may be fact; but in this there is no criterion of judging mental ability.

Notwithstanding his reservations he was balanced enough to recognize that his own observations were conditioned. Writing of the aboriginal language he admitted 'To an European ear the articulation seems uncommonly wild and barbarous; owing very likely, to those national prejudices every man imbibes, and perhaps cannot entirely divest himself of.' He recognized their dexterity with boats and their hunting weapons as well as their fondness for music and painting. An artist himself he appreciated the fact that the aboriginals often sat with him by the hour when he was at work.

Exploring expeditions were a minor theme of life in the colony. In 1791, 20 people including two aboriginals set out with the Governor. Each man had provisions for 10 days, a gun, a blanket and a water canteen. Every man but the Governor carried a knapsack, on which was slung a cooking kettle and a hatchet. One of the party vividly described their arduous life,

. . . the march begins at sunrise, and with occasional halts continues until about an hour and a half before sunset. It is necessary to stop thus early to prepare for passing the night, for toil here ends not with the march. Instead of the cheering blaze, the welcoming landlord, and the long bill of fare, the traveller has now to collect his fuel, to erect his wigwam, to fetch water, and to broil his morsel of salt pork. Let him then lie down and, if it be summer, try whether the effect of fatigue is sufficiently powerful to overcome the bites and stings of the myriads of sandflies and mosquitoes which buzz around him.

Governor Phillip, speared at Manly Cove. Unknown artist. BM(NH)

Recordings of aboriginal life, from the Watling collection. BM(NH)

Aboriginal striking fish.
Unknown artist.

Group on the north shore.
By Thomas Watling.

Travelling through barren country they reached the Hawkesbury River, to find it 'as wide as the Thames at Putney'. At that point over 300 feet wide, the river ran between high, tree-covered banks. Hindered by an impassable creek the explorers then 'scrambled with infinite toil and difficulty to the top of a neighbouring mountain', to discover that they had been going in an opposite direction to the one they believed they had been taking. Wearily they returned to the river, and retraced their tracks up it once more to be faced again by another impassable creek.

The two aboriginals who accompanied the expedition were soon thoroughly bored by it and indicated as much by constantly inquiring 'Where's Rose Hill?' The hope that they would be more familiar with the country was dashed when they seemed surprised by the river, and they sorely tried the patience of their white companions, by their mirth at their clumsy and painful progress. At other times their high spirits and imitations were a welcome diversion.

Baffled and disappointed the party had returned to Rose Hill. No wonder Phillip found that these trips had 'lately been declined by most of those who were at first induced to engage in them from motives of curiosity'. Nevertheless, as a result of these explorations, it became clearer how the colony was situated. To the west it was barred by the Hawkesbury River, and, further beyond, by the elusive Blue Mountains which would baffle explorers for many years. Along the coast between Broken Bay and Botany Bay the sandy and arid land mostly was 'so bad as to preclude cultivation'. Only the country lying between Rose Hill and the Hawkesbury could be relied on for cultivation. The Hawkesbury area fortunately was accessible by boat from Sydney, eliminating the problem of cutting roads through the bush. In the coming years its fertile banks were to attract rich farming settlements such as Green Hills, Richmond, Windsor and Ebenezer that fed the colony. As far as Phillip was concerned, however, exploration failed to solve his urgent need for good, rich soil to produce crops quickly enough to feed the colony until store ships came from

Climbing trees. Unknown artist.

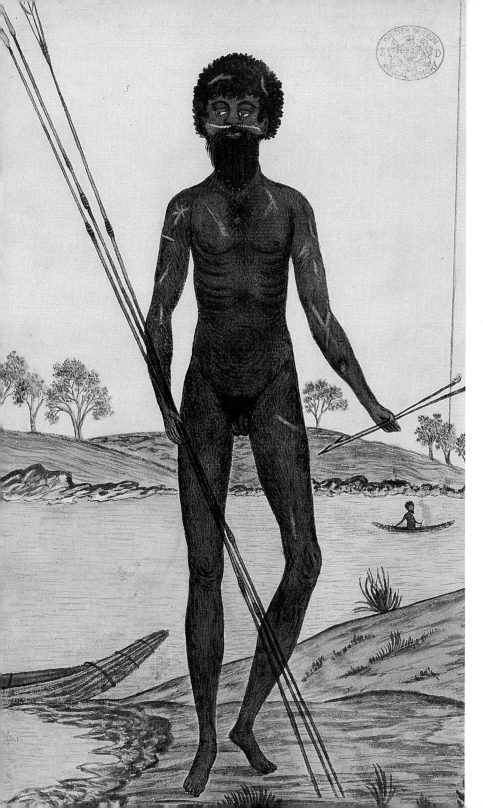

England. It was, in fact, the unexplored south-west that would reveal the good, open country so desperately sought.

The first ship of the 'Third Fleet' arrived in July 1791 and the rest of the Fleet arrived within 2 months. With it came further instructions for Phillip. Time-expired convicts were to be free to leave the settlement if they wished, but if they decided to stay they were to be given land and supplied with government rations until they were self-supporting. Some accepted this offer and a few soldiers also decided to settle. Some of the military and civil officers were already cultivating estates around Rose Hill, which had taken on a permanent air. Storehouses and barracks stood amidst rows of clay and wattle huts. There was also a barn, a granary, a blacksmith's shop and an enclosed yard for stock. A fine, broad road had been completed, from the landing place on the river to the Governor's house. A mile long and completely straight, in places it had been carried over deep gullies, which had been filled up with trunks of trees covered with earth.

A sense of accomplishment helped to soften disappointments though it was not without mixed felings that one inhabitant wrote, 'In a colony which contains only a few hundred hovels built of twigs and mud, we feel consequntial enough already to talk of a treasury, an admiralty, a public library, and many other similar edifices, which are to form part of a magnificent square.' Phillip, though in persistent ill-health, had established his colony. Granted leave of absence he sailed from Sydney on 11 December 1792. With him went 'involuntarily and cheerfully' and with great trust, two aboriginals who had become attached to him. He believed that his return to England was now the greatest service he could render the colony for as he wrote, 'It will put it in my power to shew what may and what may not be expected from it'.

The first account of the colony, *The Voyage of Governor Phillip to Botany Bay*, was published in London in 1789. It was based on a number of sources including

Chief Camergal. Unknown artist.

official papers, and two of its chapters were devoted to the animal life of New South Wales. Between duties officials in the colony found time to explore and write about the settlement, but also to try and describe its many novel features. Though Phillip's duties were arduous and his time occupied in writing official despatches to the Home Office in England, he was trained to observe. An amateur naturalist, but apparently no artist himself, he managed to find about him enough talent to make sketches and illustrations, and animals as well as plant specimens were sent to influential people in England with increasing frequency. In a letter to the Secretary of State, Lord Sydney, he wrote,

The Commander of the armed tender 'Supply' has an animal in charge which is known in England by the name of Kangaroo, and which I hope will live to be delivered by your Lordship, for the purpose of being sent to His Majesty. I have taken this liberty, as it is not known that any animal of this kind has hitherto been seen in England . . .

On his return to England he took with him a collection of plants and animals including four live kangaroos and several dingoes, or native dogs.

Other accounts of life in New South Wales were published very quickly. In 1789 Watkin Tench also published *A Narrative of the Expedition to Botany Bay*. In 1793 he followed up this first book with *A Complete Account of the Settlement at Port Jackson*. In his narratives Tench included several descriptions of Australian wildlife, including the first account of an emu. Having confirmed the great variety of beautiful birds he nominated 'the bird which principally claims attention' to be 'a species of ostrich approaching nearer to the emu of South America than any other we know of'.

Tench also drew attention to the fact that 'To beasts of prey we are utter strangers, nor have we yet any cause to believe that they exist in the country'. Another marine in the First Fleet, David Collins, became Judge-Advocate and Secretary of the new settlement, and later Lieutenant-Governor of Van Diemen's Land. It was not until 10 years later that

Spiny anteater *Tachyglossus aculeatus*. By Thomas Watling, accompanied by detailed notes by surgeon John White. BM(NH)

the first volume of his long and careful narrative was published as *An Account of the English colony in New South Wales (1798)*.

The naval surgeon with the First Fleet, John White (1756–1832) was another amateur naturalist who went with Phillip on two exploring expeditions. From the time he joined the Fleet, White kept a journal and collected specimens and drawings in the colony. Some of these were possibly included in *The Voyage of Governor Phillip to Botany Bay*. His account was published as a *Journal of a Voyage to New South Wales* (London 1790). It had many engraved illustrations, mostly of the natural history of the colony, based on specimens sent to England by White. The book was such a great success with German, Swedish and French editions following, that White prepared a manuscript for a second book. Before he left the colony in December 1794 he had sent back many specimens and drawings, many made by his convict servant, Thomas Watling. White's project for a second book came to nothing but the drawings he assembled for its illustration are possibly those which form the so-called 'Port Jackson Artist' Collection which came into the possession of Joseph Banks and are now in the British Museum (Natural History). This intriguing collection of 69 paintings, mostly of natural history around Port Jackson, is mainly of unsigned work. It was, however, a common practice for artists and collectors to copy whatever drawings of novel scenes or objects they could come by, often not even knowing who had drawn the original.

The Governor who replaced Phillip was John Hunter (1737–1821), who had been second captain of the *Sirius* and had, at that time, also held a dormant commission as governor. An active explorer, Hunter had surveyed and charted Port Jackson, Broken Bay and Botany Bay in 1788. He had taken the *Sirius* to the Cape of Good Hope before it was wrecked at Norfolk Island on its way to China. No stranger to shipwrecks, Hunter had spent his enforced stay making a detailed survey of the island. As Governor he continued to encourage exploration and make extensive journeys on his own.

John Hunter (1737–1821), second captain of the *Sirius* and second Governor of New South Wales. Frontpiece to Hunter's *Journal*.

Hunter governed a population of 3211, 31 of whom were civil officers. There were 1908 convicts and the rest were soldiers and officers of the New South Wales Corps or time-expired convicts. By this time civil and military officers were farming huge land grants with the help of convict labour, and they owned most of the livestock. Hunter discovered that private enterprise had begun to supplant government-organized activity and the government, in fact, was faced with a labour shortage. Many ex-convicts were being employed in the quickly growing and very lucrative sealing industry. Conscientious and friendly, but as a naval man without much support against his mainly military adversaries, Hunter became increasingly powerless in the faction-fighting that developed as a struggle for control of the colony's resources.

Hunter was a member of the Royal Society and a keen student of natural history. He kept in touch with Banks and sent many specimens, descriptions and drawings to England. Hunter, who enjoyed rambling on his own, was closely associated with the discovery of several of Australia's most unique animals, including the lyrebird, koala, wombat and platypus. One of the many fine natural history specimens that he sent to England, a platypus, was acquired by Newcastle Museum. He was also a very pleasing artist, and before becoming Governor had published *An Historical Journal of the Transactions at Port Jackson and Norfolk Island* (1973), largely illustrated by his own work.

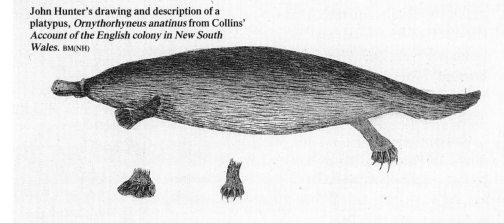

John Hunter's drawing and description of a platypus, *Ornythorhyneus anatinus* from Collins' *Account of the English colony in New South Wales.* BM(NH)

AN AMPHIBIOUS ANIMAL of the MOLE KIND.

which Inhabits the Banks of the fresh water Lagoons in New South Wales, its fore feet are evidently their principal assistance in Swimming & their hind feet having the Claws extending beyond the Webb't part are useful in burrowing.

Few artists travelled to Australia. Indeed, few professionals had the money or the opportunities to study the land and its people as closely as those who went there on government business. This gap was filled by the many sailors and convicts who turned out to have artistic talents. Like today's newspaper photographers they met the demand for pictures that confirmed the stories of animals and plants never seen before. One of the most outstanding and professional was the convict artist Thomas Watling (1762–?).

Watling was born in Scotland, obviously trained in the former style of painting and well educated. He was transported to New South Wales at his own request, for suspected forgery. He had helped to avert a mutiny before he left England, but received no recognition and then made an unsuccessful attempt to escape at Cape Town. When he reached Sydney in 1792 he was assigned as a servant to surgeon John White who worked him hard producing drawings. Watling, who was an excellent artist, did not enjoy his association with White whom he described as 'a very mercenary, sordid person'. When White left the colony Watling may have been assigned to David Collins, who in his first book used engraved illustrations made from sketches by Watling. His work included delicate landscapes, some vivid studies of aboriginals and a great many natural history drawings of birds, insects, fishes and mammals.

Watling's irreverent mind is clear in his series of *Letters from an exile at Botany Bay to his Aunt in Dumfries,* published in Scotland probably in 1794, which is a rare account of early colonial life from outside the privileged circle of administration. After serving only 5 of his 14 year sentence Watling was given an absolute pardon by Governor Hunter and returned to Scotland, only to find himself again under suspicion of forging. The last that is known of him is that seriously ill, and in desperate circumstances in London, he was aided later by ex-governor Hunter.

The work he produced in Australia is in the 'Watling Collection' held by the British Museum (Natural History). This collection of over 500 drawings was compiled

Birds of New South Wales. By Thomas Watling. BM(NH)

Yellow-tailed black cockatoo
Calyptorhynchus funereus

64

Eastern whipbird
Psophodes olivaceus

Lambert's Drawing K. 47.

Coach-whip Flycatcher Supp.

Thomas Watling, delt.

One half the Natural size, Native name Wau-wau.

This Bird from a single note resembling the crack of a Coachmans
Whip, is called the Coach Whip, Flycatcher Latham Syn Supp.d 2.p.222.

Cicada-bird
Edoliisoma tenirostre

Velvet faced Crow Lathams MS

apparently before 1794 around Port Jackson. They are clearly the work of several artists but 123 drawings are signed by Watling and some others would seem to be in his style. Because some of these works have been annotated by John White, it is most likely that the entire collection was originally made and taken to England by White.

From 1800–06 New South Wales was governed by Phillip Gidley King, a naval officer who had also arrived with the First Fleet. Many new settlements were set up in this period. King, who had originally administered the settlement at Norfolk Island, set up a colony at the Coal River (Newcastle) in 1802. Further settlements were set up in Tasmania. In 1802 a settlement to be established at Port Phillip (now Melbourne) was diverted to the River Derwent to the south of Van Diemen's Land. This was Hobart Town where Adolarius Humphrey, a mineralogist appointed to this expedition by Banks, built the first house. In 1804 King founded a settlement at Port Dalrymple (later Launceston).

Though he sent out several land expeditions, King was always more aware of the sea. Perhaps because of his naval background he took a spacious view of the Pacific. He unsuccessfully urged the establishment of a settlement in New Zealand but persuaded a hesitant government in London of the value of retaining a colony at Norfolk Island, especially as a base for British whaling ships, whose activities in the Southern Pacific made them frequent and welcome visitors at Hobart and Sydney.

Diamond python
Morelia spilota.
Unknown artist.
Port Jackson Artist Collection.
BM(NH)

Lucky Bay. By William Westall. NMM

Chapter 7
Maritime exploration

For 25 years after its foundation, the New South Wales settlement remained shut in between the Blue Mountains and the sea. Geographers as well as naturalists were increasingly curious to know more of the hinterland of the continent, an interior which in its extent was nearly equal to the land mass of Europe itself. Naturally there was speculation about what would be found there. There was still a possibility that the continent might be divided into as yet undiscovered islands by waterways running between the north and south. Alternatively there might be an inland lake or sea connected to an entrance at some part of the yet unexplored coastline.

A second phase of maritime exploration in Australia began with the attempt to settle these questions. The man whose name was to be associated with these explorations was Lincolnshire born Matthew Flinders (1774–1814) who came to New South Wales in 1795 in HMS *Reliance* with Governor Hunter. The ship's surgeon, George Bass, was also from Lincolnshire and the pair were to waste no time in beginning their explorations. First they went on an expedition to Botany Bay in a tiny 8-foot boat, aptly named the *Tom Thumb,* and by following the George's River, discovered some open country that allowed Hunter to establish a settlement at the place he named Bankstown. They then went further south than anyone had gone to Port Hacking and Lake Illawarra. Their enquiries had to be abandoned while the *Reliance* went to Cape Town to fetch livestock for the colony. Immediately on his return Bass failed in an attempt to find a way across the Blue Mountains, but returning to the sea and driving south again he discovered coal in the coastal cliffs within 20 miles of Sydney.

Governor Hunter, who himself had wide experience of these coastal waters, was anxious to test his theory that there might be a channel between the mainland and Van Diemen's Land. If this was so it would greatly simplify navigation to Port Jackson, for shipping could cross the south of the continent without having to sweep further south around the extremity of Van Diemen's Land, as was the usual practice. In December 1797 Bass went south-west in a whaleboat with a crew of six. He went as far as Wilson's Promontory and Western Port but his supplies threatened to run out and he returned to Sydney convinced that the tides and currents he had met with indicated that Van Diemen's Land was indeed separated from the mainland. His friend Flinders later wrote admiringly of this voyage in a 28 foot open boat that '600 miles of coast, mostly in a boisterous climate, was explored, perhaps without its equal in the annals of maritime history.'

The following year (1798) Bass and Flinders sailed right around Van Diemen's Land, thereby establishing that it was an island. Governor King later named the channel that separated it from the mainland after Bass. The discoveries they made of Port Dalrymple at the north of Van Diemen's Land and the Derwent River (Hobart) at the south, prepared the way for settlements in these areas.

Flinders had a brief opportunity to examine parts of the Queensland coast before he returned to England with the *Reliance* in 1800.

The same year that Flinders left Australia the Admiralty sent off the 60 ton *Lady Nelson*. Joseph Banks had secured the command for Lieutenant Grant. The time had come for a thorough survey of the coastline of the continent. On the orders of the Secretary of State, Lord Portland, the *Lady Nelson* was to prosecute the discovery and survey of the unknown parts of the coast of New Holland. The *Lady Nelson* was an ingenious experimental ship designed with inshore exploration in mind. She had three unique sliding keels which could be raised to allow her to enter shallow water. On the outward voyage to New South Wales, Grant was directed to try the new route through the strait discovered by Bass and Flinders.

Matthew Flinders (1774–1814), navigator and explorer. By De Courcy-Jones, miniature on ivory.
NPG

The influence of Banks was clear. Grant was to collect specimens of seeds, plants, animals and minerals as he went and was to sow the seeds of fruit trees and vegetables wherever he went ashore, for the benefit of future vessels. The pattern set by the *Endeavour* was echoed in the instruction that a collector or naturalist would join the vessel at Sydney to whom Grant was to give his assistance. The naturalist's collections and journals were to be returned either to the Home Office or to the Royal Society.

The *Lady Nelson* was first sent to survey the south and south-west coast of the mainland and on the way to visit Western Port and the islands in Bass Strait. At Sydney the botanist George Caley had joined the ship. Caley, who had recently arrived in the colony, owed his appointment to Banks also. Grant made his first landfall at Jervis Bay where he found a great variety of insects, and heard a 'Laughing Bird' (kookaburra) for the first time. He moved on to name Churchill Island, where a rare cockatoo, the gang-gang, was shot but preserved to be painted later. At the end of the voyage, Caley, who had made a collection at Jervis Bay, caused a row by refusing to give it up. It is some indication of the rivalry and competition that accompanied collecting that Caley was suspicious that the Governor might use his specimens as gifts or associate his own name with their discovery.

On his second expedition grant was sent north to survey the entrance to the Coal River and report on the soil and natural products of a region where Governor King intended to make a new settlement (Newcastle). A miner, John Platt, was sent with Grant and they were accompanied by a small colonial schooner *Francis* to be loaded with the coal that had been found in abundance. They returned with a load of coal, which was later shipped to India, and a favourable report on the soil and local products. They also brought back some new species of plants and some specimens of birds that were sent to Banks. On her return the *Lady Nelson* was allowed to continue its interrupted survey of Bass Strait, and also to take special note of the prospects in that area for catching seals,

now commercially valuable for their pelts and oil. Caley's place in this expedition was taken by the artist and naturalist, John Lewin. On her next voyage the *Lady Nelson* discovered the spacious harbour of Port Phillip, later the site of Melbourne.

Back in England, Matthew Flinders had been actively seeking support to return to Australia. He turned to Banks, who was impressed by Flinders' charting and perhaps by two other circumstances. Flinders came from Lincolnshire where Banks had his estates, and Flinders already had some important experience in the Pacific. Some 10 years earlier, Captain William Bligh, who was a protégé of Banks, had proposed a thorough survey of the coastline to Banks, but Bligh had then set off on his second breadfruit voyage in the *Providence* (1791–93). Flinders had been a midshipman on this voyage and had learned from and admired Bligh's formidable skill in navigation. Because Bligh had been master of Cook's ship, the *Resolution,* on his third voyage to the Pacific, Flinders proudly claimed through these links to be a disciple of Cook.

It was a matter of some concern that so many years after Cook's first voyage it was still not known whether the Dutch-explored west coast and the British colonized east coast were, in fact, one land mass. Flinders achieved his ambition. In February 1801 he was appointed commander of the HMS *Investigator* (334 tons). He was instructed to make a complete examination of the Australian coastline, in particular 'the Unknown Coast' east across the Great Australian Bight. The voyage was to make Flinders's reputation as a navigator.The same year his *Observations on the Coasts of Van Diemen's Land, on Bass's Strait and its Islands, and on part of the Coast of N.S.W.* was published in London.

Echoes of Cook persisted in the fitting out of Flinders's expedition. The *Investigator* carried a distinguished group of civilian scientists in the tradition established by Cook's expedition. This voyage was also to have particular consequences for scientific enquiry. The eminent botanist, Sir Joseph Dalton Hooker, pronounced that as far as botany was concerned this expedition was 'the most important in its results ever undertaken, and hence marks an epoch in the history of that science . Flinders's group included an astronomer, Crosley (whose inability to finish the voyage threw an added burden on Flinders), a landscape painter William Westall (1781–1850) who was a student of the Royal Academy School, a botanical painter Ferdinand Bauer (1760–1826), and the naturalist Robert Brown (1773–1858). There was also a miner, John Allen, to collect geological samples and Brown had, as assistant, a gardener Peter Good, and a portable greenhouse to preserve the plant collection. The salaries of this group give some indication of their importance. The annual salary of the gardener and miner was £105, the draughtsman £315 and the naturalist £420. The naturalist and draughtsman were each allowed a servant.

Flinders sighted the Australian coast at Cape Leeuwin. A previous British expedition under Captain Vancouver on its way to the north-east Pacific in 1791 had discovered the fine harbour of King

George's Sound (now Albany, Western Australia). With the aid of Vancouver's charts, Flinders landed at and named Fowlers Bay. From there he sailed east to survey and chart the entire length of the south coast of Australia. Flinders discovered and named Port Lincoln, Spencers Gulf and Gulf St Vincent (South Australia) as well as exploring and naming Kangaroo Island in Bass Strait. He also made frequent landfalls 'in order that the naturalists may have time to range about and collect the produce of the earth'.

At the place he named Encounter Bay Flinders met with the ship *Le Géographe,* one of a two-ship French scientific expedition under Captain Nicholas Baudin. Both Baudin's ships *Le Géographe* and *Le Naturaliste* anchored at Sydney shortly after Flinders had arrived there, and were given an official welcome. The French were impressed to find Sydney functioning busily as a port, and already well established in the sea routes of the Pacific. They also discovered a colony more wholesome and civilized than the wretched penitentiary they had been anticipating.

Confined by its intractable hinterland, Sydney faced automatically to the sea and the French were equally surprised to find ships in Port Jackson from many parts of the world. Noting that the American flag was to be seen in the harbour throughout their visit, they listed the presence of British whaling ships, a vessel preparing to set off for South America, and another bound for the fur trade on the north-west coast of America. Some convict transport ships, having unloaded their live cargo, were bound for China and cargoes of tea, but there was evidence of a local trade beginning as ships were loaded with colonial coal and timber and sent to India and the Cape of Good Hope. There were a number of small colonial boats shuttling to the sealing islands of the Bass Strait, or fitting out for nearby Pacific Islands to load

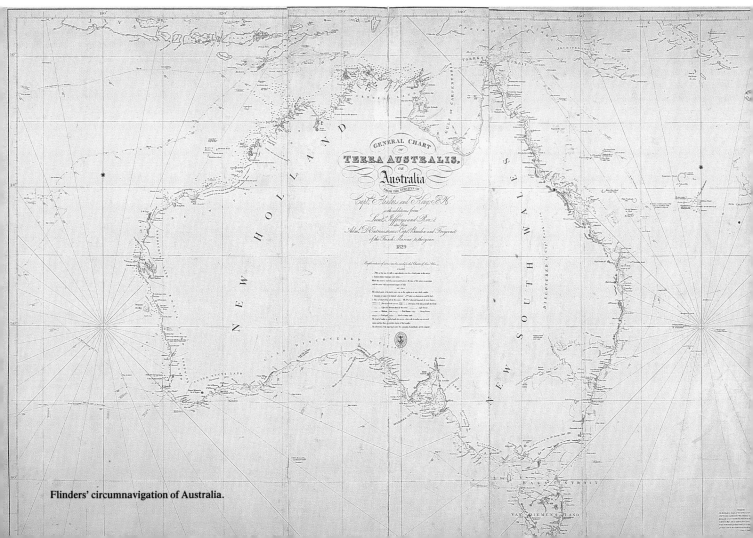

Flinders' circumnavigation of Australia.

with pork, a welcome addition to the colony's restricted diet and a meat that salted well to replenish visiting ships.

Shipbuilding yards along the harbour foreshores were busy repairing ships or building small vessels from local timber. 'All these operations, all these movements of ships,' wrote a member of the French expedition Francois Peron, 'gave an appearance of importance and activity that we were not at all expecting to find on these shores hitherto unknown in Europe and our interest redoubled with our admiration.'

At Sydney, however, there was a strong suspicion of this French interest, and their motives. Only a few hours after the French had sailed, Governor King heard a rumour that they intended to make a settlement at Storm Bay on the east side of Van Diemen's Land. He immediately sent two expeditions from Sydney, one to take possession officially at Storm Bay Passage and the other to do the same at Port Phillip or King Island in Bass Strait. In doing so King was actually anticipating the intentions of the British government. An expedition of two ships, the *Calcutta* and *Ocean,* had already left England on its way to establish a settlement at Port Phillip (now Melbourne) at the western approach to Bass Strait. This new settlement was intended to act as a depot for the commercially important sealing industry in Bass Strait, and at the same time prevent the permanent arrival of 'troublesome neighbours' for Port Jackson. In the event this expedition, finding Port Phillip unsuitable for settlement, went on to Van Diemen's Land where Hobart was established instead.

Three months after having reached Sydney, Flinders set out northwards from Port Jackson in July 1802 on his way to explore the east (Queensland) coast, the Torres Strait and the Gulf of Carpentaria in the north. Now sailing in Cook's *Endeavour* tracks, Flinders wrote, 'He reaped the harvest of discovery, but the gleanings of the field remain to be gathered.'

Intending to head for Torres Strait at the northern extremity of the continent before the onset of the monsoon season, Flinders

decided to leave the coast at Broad Sound. To do so he had, like Cook, to sail eastward through the hazardous Barrier Reef. Trapped among the treacherous coral reefs, it took Flinders 14 days sailing and searching by day and dragging anchors by night before he found the channel now named Flinders Passage. Having been with Bligh when he found a way through the hardly less difficult Torres Strait, Flinders intended to find the quickest and safest route through the Strait. The route he discovered, by way of 'Pandora's Entrance', allowed the Strait to be navigated in 3 days. His charts made the previously treacherous passage relatively safe and allowed nearly 40 days to be cut off the sailing time from Port Jackson to the Cape of Good Hope.

By the time he reached the Gulf of Carpentaria a survey of the *Investigator* showed her to be so rotten she could hardly remain afloat and it was clear that Flinders must return to Port Jackson. He nevertheless finished the charting of the Gulf of Carpentaria and being determined to attempt his ambition to circumnavigate the continent he took the gamble of returning by way of the western coast.

Robert Brown (1773 – 1858), botanist.
By H W Piccersgill, oil on canvas.
LS

Eight members of the crew died of fever at Kupang in Timor but Flinders brought the *Investigator* to anchor in Port Jackson on 9 June 1803 after navigating the Australian Bight in the depths of winter.

As the *Investigator* needed extensive repairs, Flinders, anxious to obtain another ship and finish his work, left Sydney as a passenger in HMS *Porpoise* for England. When she sank on a reef on the east coast, Flinders, in a brilliant achievement, navigated her open cutter over 700 miles back to Port Jackson to get help for those who had been marooned. He then left Sydney again in the tiny and dangerously unfit schooner *Cumberland* (29 tons) and nursed her successfully through the Torres Straits, struggling as far as Mauritius where he had to seek help for his foundering ship. He arrived at the French colony of Mauritius only a day after Baudin in *Le Géographe* had left there to return to France. Flinders was unaware that war had broken out again between England and France and as a consequence he was held at Mauritius under arrest until 1810. He occupied his frustrating captivity in revising his charts and maps. Flinders returned to England, broken in health, to labour on his book *A Voyage to Terra Australis* which was published the day before he died in 1814.

Flinders made the last epic voyage of discovery in the South Pacific and completed the outline of Terra Australis Incognita. A brilliant navigator and hydrographer, he left charts so meticulous that they were trusted in World War II. His intention to make 'so accurate an investigation of the shores of Terra Australis that no future voyage to this country should be necessary' was totally achieved and he was justified in concluding that 'nothing of importance should have been left for future discoveries upon any part of these extensive coasts'.

Flinders's maritime achievement was paralleled by the equally brilliant botanical and artistic results of the *Investigator's* voyage. The botanist, Robert Brown (1773–1858) had been appointed to the expedition only after Mungo Park had refused. Through his connection with the Linnean Society Brown, originally a military surgeon's mate, was one of the most important of Banks's protégés. The tall and imposing son of a Scottish minister, he was to leave a lasting influence on botanical science. He prepared for the expedition by a thorough study of the Australian plants in Banks's collection.

With the help of Peter Good, and at times of Ferdinand Bauer, Brown made an extensive collection during Flinders's voyage, but when the group was returning to England he lost part of his material in the wreck of the *Porpoise.* However, Brown and Bauer had remained at Sydney with the bulk of their collections. Brown also went collecting in Van Diemen's Land and around Port Phillip, as well as around Sydney and in the Hunter River area. Brown and Bauer left Sydney in 1805 in the *Investigator* and during the voyage Brown had to secure his precious collections of over 3000 specimens, of which more than half were unknown, from the all pervading damp of the still unseaworthy ship.

Some 30 years after collections had been made on the *Endeavour,* there was still no system determined on the arrangement or classification of Australian flora. The uniqueness of these plants left botanists without any point of comparison. The exploring botanist found that 'Whole tribes of plants which first seem familiar . . . prove on a nearer examination, total strangers, with other configurations, other economy, and other qualities; not only the species that present themselves are new, but most of the genera, and even natural orders.' Brown attempted a radical new approach. During his collecting he would select a range of plants in various stages of development as well as in their mature state. As a result he was able to classify them in a system depending on the analysis of the anatomy and physiology of their parts. He engaged Bauer in making detailed illustrations of floral and seed structure that helped to fortify the reasons for his approach.

Plants drawn by Ferdinand Bauer on the voyage of the Investigator.
BM(NH)

Wild nutmeg
Myristica insipida

Cycad
Cycas media

Brown had a lifelong connection with the Linnean Society as its clerk, librarian and as its president and vice-president, but his only major work on Australian plants *Prodomus Florae Novae Hollandiae et Insulae Van Diemen* published in 1810 supported the 'natural system' of classification of Jussieu against the Linnean system. This departure was one of the most seminal influences in botanical science and helped to revitalize this science. An appendix, 'general remarks, geographical and systematical, on the botany of Terra Australis', that Brown contributed to Flinders's *Voyage* (1814), supports Brown's original contribution to the science of plant geography.

Brown was held in high regard by his contemporaries. Kind and generous, he was reserved in the company of all but his close friends to whom he revealed a dry wit. In 1810 he became librarian to Joseph Banks, who left him an annuity of £200, a lease of his house at Soho Square and a life interest in his collections. In 1827 the collections were transferred to a new department in the British Museum under Brown's personal direction. His links with Australian botany continued all his life and a supplement to his *Prodomus* was published in 1830 dealing with additional specimens collected by others. His personal collections went to the British Museum in 1876.

The artistic and graphic results of the *Investigator* voyage were to reach incredible standards in the work of Ferdinand Lukas Bauer (1760–1826). It was Joseph Banks who arranged for Austrian-born Bauer to join the *Investigator* as a botanical draughtsman. The son of the Prince of Liechtenstein's court painter, Bauer's magnificent drawings of plants and animals on which he was then engaged for Oxford professor John Sibthorpe were published as *Flora Graeca* (London, 1806–40) after his return from Australia.

Crow's ash
Flindersia australis

Silver box
Eucalyptus pruinosa

Animals drawn by Ferdinand Bauer
on the voyage of the *Investigator*.

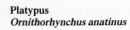

Koalas
Phascolarctus cinereus

Platypus
Ornithorhynchus anatinus

Bauer was an able botanist and worked closely with Robert Brown helping him collect his specimens. Also in co-operation with Brown's investigations Bauer made highly magnified studies of the parts of flowers and plant organs which were invaluable in the analysis of plant structure.

Despite the perhaps more unfavourable conditions in the decrepit *Investigator,* Bauer emulating Parkinson, managed to make 1000 drawings of plants and 200 of animals by August 1803. By the time he returned to England in 1805 he had made 2073 drawings of which some 1540 were of Australian plants and the remainder were of plants from Norfolk Island, Timor and the Cape, and of animals from Australia and Norfolk Island. These were all pencil sketches which Bauer finished later with the guidance of his colour key. His friend Robert Brown wrote, 'Considering his minute accuracy the number of drawings he has made is astonishing.'

On his return Bauer was commissioned by the Admiralty to complete a number of watercolour drawings which Banks stipulated should be supervised by Robert Brown. Unable to find craftsmen capable of engraving or colouring his plates according to his own perfectionist standards, Bauer attempted to do even this work himself. Ten of Bauer's plates were included in the atlas accompanying Flinders's *A Voyage to Terra Australis* (London 1814). Bauer intended to publish much of his work and in 1813 issued his *Illustrationes Florae Novae Hollandiae* which ran to only 15 exquisite plates before the project was abandoned. After failure of this series, Bauer returned to his native Austria in 1814 where he completed his Australian drawings. Though some of Bauer's drawings were used to illustrate botanical works, most of them were never published. A major part of them were presented by the Admiralty to the British Museum (Natural History).

Bauer and his brother Franz, a botanical artist at Kew Gardens for 50 years, were 'two of the finest draughtsmen in the whole history of botanic art'. Ferdinand's combination of detailed accuracy with artistic judgement produced work of

Blue swimming crab
Portunus pelagicus

Weedy sea dragon
Phyllopteryx

unparalleled quality and charm. The German poet, Goethe, said of Bauer's drawings that they 'revealed that the service both of art and science, though difficult, was still possible.'

William Westall (1781–1850) who travelled with the *Investigator* as landscape artist, had been studying at the Royal Academy Schools when he joined the expedition at the age of 19. As part of the official record of the voyage Westall produced many of the earliest drawings of the Australian coast. He drew many pencil and pencil-and-wash landscapes at the places where the *Investigator* touched the coast, as well as some extremely fine pencil coast profiles which were used as illustrative aids to navigation in atlases. To the latter he brought a new sense of dimension and clarity.

Young Westall, in search of the exotic, was disappointed with the Australian coastal land he had to work with and began to turn his attention to precise studies of the vegetation, perhaps influenced by Bauer, and to studies of aboriginals. When the *Porpoise* was wrecked many of Westall's drawings were 'wetted and partly destroyed', but were taken to England where, at the suggestion of Banks, they were restored successfully.

Westall had seized his opportunity after the wreck of the *Porpoise* to go travelling and sketching in the more romantic lands of China and India, but on his return to England he was commissioned by the Admiralty to complete pictures to illustrate Flinders's *Voyage*. Several oil paintings made for the Admiralty suggest that Westall had become intrigued by light and atmosphere and was attempting to incorporate their effects in his work. He became a prolific artist, producing many works for popular regional and travel works, travelling later in Madeira and the West Indies. He exhibited with the Royal Academy, London, many times and was an associate of the Academy. At the time of his death he was at work on a painting of the wreck of the *Porpoise*.

Kangaroo Island. By William Westall. NMM

Somerset House, home of the Royal Society of London (1780–1857).

Chapter 8
Back in Britain

News of the distant colony gradually filtered back to Britain and stirred up interest in this new area of the world. It was a feature of the later 18th century, believing itself on the brink of a new era of civilization, that the passion for discovery was happy to be diverted into 'undertakings to which avarice let no incentive and fortune annexed no reward'. At the very time in which more was being learned about Australia, a liberal spirit of curiosity waited ready for revelations, and associations were being formed for the promotion of scientific enquiry.

Interest in the 'non-descript' productions of New Holland stimulated hundreds of drawings of Australian plants and animals during the early years of settlement. Over 1000 works of botanical and zoological value are known to have been produced in New South Wales before the turn of the century. Most of the drawings found their way to England. Some were used to illustrate voyage and travel books relating to Australia, other books and journals associated with the study of natural history. Early interest was in natural curios rather than landscape drawings though eventually drawings of the picturesque beauties of the Australian landscape with suitably exotic additions were also produced in great numbers.

Public interest in New Holland was catered for in several ways. The first available information was in the published illustrated journals of officials. Their published accounts were followed by issues of specialist interest such as the *Naturalists' Pocket Magazine* (1799) that included early illustrations of plants and animals from New South Wales. Under the stimulus of novelty these generally well educated administrators found time to write, sketch and collect. The flood of lavish serial natural history volumes produced at this time, in which Australian species sometimes dominated, eventually glutted the available market. In an age of patronage colonial administrators were more than eager to feed this curiosity, happy to draw themselves to the favourable attention of influential people and officials in London.

Governor Phillip was quick to send early samples of seeds, flax and emu feathers to Banks requesting that he share the seeds with Lord Sydney at the Home Office and 'Mr Nepean'. He also sent a preserved kangaroo and an emu skin for Lord Sydney and forwarded some Lord Howe Island birds to Lady Chatham. Several of the colonial governors were themselves members of the Royal Society, so that information flowed directly to this source from the colony. The Society often directed and encouraged widespread searches, being just as concerned to discover resources with some profitable commercial application.

In the early 19th century a great deal of intellectual energy was being channelled into an explosion of interest in natural history. Previously this had been a field dominated by eccentrics and antiquarians, but it became fashionable for the wealthy upper classes to amass collections and libraries, an innocent combination that filled their leisure and helped to advance knowledge. The investigation of the Australian environment coincided with this development and gave an impetus to enquiry, and especially to the making of collections. For the first few decades after

the arrival of the First Fleet a flood of specimens went back to England to satisfy the craze for this form of 'national amusement'.

A steady flow of samples was available in the early years but the trade in New South Wales in seeds, live plants and animals was

'The Kangaroo.'
Engraving from *the Voyage of Governor Phillip to Botany Bay*.

to assume huge proportions. Gentlemen travellers as well as officers assiduously made their own collections, often buying specimens, and convicts spent their time collecting to sell to visitors and to those leaving the colony. Natural history collections were frequently offered for sale in the *Sydney Gazette*. In one issue in 1809 a 'superb small beautiful collection of insects', five emus and a collection of parrots as well as several of botanical seeds, were advertised. It was a profitable trade. When one visitor to the colony tried to expand his own hasty collection with purchased specimens he found the prices too high. To his chagrin a far-sighted ship's officer was able to exchange his hogshead of rum for any number of kangaroos, parrots, opossums and shells.

In London some enterprising individuals were quick to cater to the same interest in novelty at a more general level and it was not long before some of the extraordinary Australian wildlife went on display to the British public. The first live kangaroo was being exhibited within a short time of the colony's foundation. It was advertised in the *Ladies' Magazine* for January 1790 as

The wonderful kangaroo from Botany Bay (the only one ever brought alive to Europe). Removed from Haymarket, and now exhibited at the Lyceum, in the Strand, from eight o'clock in the morning to eight in the evening.

This amazing, beautiful, and tame Animal is about five feet in Height, of a Fawn Colour, and distinguishes itself in Shape, Make and true Symmetry of Parts, different from all other Quadrupeds. Its swiftness when pursued, is superior to the Greyhound: to enumerate its extraordinary Qualities would exceed the common limits of a Public Notice. Let it suffice to observe that the Public in General are pleased to bestow their Plaudits; the Ingenius are deighted; the Virtuoso, and Connoisseur, are taught to admire! impressing the beholder with Wonder and Astonishment, at the sight of the unparalleled animal from the Southern Hemisphere, that almost surpasses Belief; therefore Ocular Demonstration will exceed all that words can describe, or Pencil delineate . . . Admittance, One Shilling each.

London nurserymen, notably Grimwoods of Kensington and Lee and Kennedy of Hammersmith, had cultivated Australian plants from seeds from the *Endeavour* collection, some of which were to be seen 'in the highest perfection' at Hammersmith as early as 1789. One of Australia's first profitable exports was commercial trade in plants and seeds. Lee had printed his own instructions for collectors in the colony. The seeds were returned to London perfectly ripened and dried before being folded up in paper. They were packed between alternate layers of oakum, to discourage insects and then wrapped in oilskin to keep out moisture. Professional botanists were also interested in this market, and Lee advised that new plants should be selected for their beauty or for their usefulness in 'mechanics, food or physic' or for dyes, but he was interested in trees or shrubs particularly and anything that would constitute an attractive herbaceous plant.

Lee was aware that he had an eager demand to satisfy. Thanks to the

Wattle
Acacia rostellifera

advancement of horticulture and landscape gardening, and particularly the development of greenhouses, the propagation of exotic plants was a fashionable craze among the wealthy whose gardeners too, vied with one another to cultivate exotic specimens. Australian plants were seized on with interest and enthusiasm. Mimosa, or wattle, had been successfully grown in England and even before 1800 was fairly common in greenhouses. Enthusiasts such as the Dowager Lady de Clifford and Lord Viscount Lewisham were cultivating Australian plants even before 1794. The wife of the Home Secretary, the Duchess of Portland, who was in a position to benefit from all new discoveries, included this pastime among her many interests. Some idea of the interest reserved for these matters can be gathered from a letter she sent to Banks,

The Dchss of P understands the Nympheaea Nelumbo [East Indian Lotus] was introduced into England by Sir Joseph Banks, and that it never has yet Flowered in this country - The Dchss of Portland came to town from Bulstrode last night, and left her plant in a very prosperous way towards Flowering very fine; and from its forward appearance should imagine that it might blow in a few days - The Dchss thought it possible Sir J Banks might have some curiosity upon this subject which is her reason for giving him this information - at the same time she should be much Obliged to him if he would let her know what Colour she may expect the Flower to be.

The cultivation of these imported plants became comparatively widespread. In 1828 Robert Sweet, a Fellow of the Linnean Society published *Flora Australasicea: or a Selection of Handsome, or Curious Plants, Natives of New Holland, and the South Sea Islands*. His book was aimed at gardeners, rather than scientists and showed the best methods of cultivation and propagation. He selected practical rather than exotic specimens, attractive evergreen shrubs easily managed. They could be grown in the conservatory or greenhouse, but there were also many 'which will endure the cold of our climate, in the open air, with very little protection'.

The co-ordinator of many of these interests, and to some extent the promoter of many of them, was Joseph Banks. The leading role that he played in the colonisation and development of Australia almost justified the light-hearted suggestion by Linneaus that the continent should have been named Banksia. Certainly no member of English society advertised the new settlement as effectively as did Banks, whose intellectual enthusiasm for New South Wales never waned.

When James Gillray, the notorious Regency cartoonist, lampooned him in 1795 as 'The Great South Sea Caterpillar, transformed into a Bath Butterfly' he was confident his subject could be recognized by this description alone, for Sir Joseph, knighted in 1781, and by then a pundit on many issues, had gained his public reputation as a result of the voyage in the *Endeavour.* His experience and his own remarkable personal ability made Banks's network of contacts even more significant. The scope of his concerns was maintained in a huge correspondence where nothing was too trivial for his personal attention.

Sir Joseph Banks, President of the Royal Society. By Thomas Philips, oil on canvas.
NFC

Cartoon satirising Banks's rise to prominence. By James Gillray. RNK

His was a powerful interest, exerted unofficially as a confidant of the King and as a friend and adviser to many of the country's ministers and administrators. A trustee of the British Museum, he was a member, often honorary, of a large number of societies and academies.

As unofficial director of the King's Gardens at Kew, Banks was to co-ordinate a complex imperial effort. Kew Gardens, with its ornate gardens and follies, was a royal favourite. This London garden also played an important part in the early development of Australia. The Royal Family were showered with gifts of live plants and animals from the new colony which were housed at Kew Gardens. Kew had been conceived as a purely pleasure garden but Banks turned it into a serious scientific institution. As he reminded Governor Hunter (1797),

I trust, good sir, that when you make your excursions, or when you send parties into new districts, you will not forget that Kew Gardens is the first in Europe, and that its Royal Master and Mistress never fail to receive personal satisfaction from every plant introduced there from foreign parts when it comes to perfection.

So many unusual Australian plants were raised and flowered at Kew for the first time that a separate building was provided. The Botany Bay House, as it became known, was for many years a special attraction.

Banks's ambition, however, was to turn Kew into a storehouse for every known plant. He used his interest with the Admiralty to provide special facilities for the return of specimens to England, and he was equally interested in sending useful plants to the colony. Few ships left

England for New South Wales without seed, and sometimes carried plants in pots to be added to the horticultural wealth of the colony.

As amateur sources were unequal to satisfying the demand, Banks sent collectors out to all corners of the world, many of them to Australia. Most of them had been trained as gardeners on estates or at Kew. George Caley was sent to New South Wales in 1800. He tried his patron Banks sorely by his truculence and quarrelsomeness, and Banks wrote of him that 'Had he been born a gentleman, he would have been shot long ago in a duel'. As the first of many consignments Caley sent Banks a box of dried plant specimens, a box of living plants, 238 packages of seeds and 65 waratah pods as well as other specimens that included almost 80 bird skins.

The Royal Gardens at Kew. BM(NH)

The study of botany dominated the early scientific association with Australia. In the same year as the foundation of the colony at Botany Bay, a scientific society devoted to the study of botany, the Linnean Society, was founded in London. Its president James Edward Smith was a close friend of Banks. This Society took a keen interest in Australian flora and as early as 1793 Smith published his *Specimen of the Botany of New Holland.*

Banks was also to have a major influence in many areas of British science. The plant material he and Solander had returned with in the *Endeavour* had confused and troubled botanists. The result was a stimulus to taxonomic botany, or the classifying and systematizing of species. The consequences were the same for zoology, though changes in thinking took longer to come about. Zoology was an area in which it was more difficult to organize evidence. It was hard a hard area for an amateur, zoological studies were not so organized and specimens were hard to obtain and preserve.

Conditioned to a preference for arbitrary systems, it was profoundly disturbing to be faced with reports of animals which could not be fitted into the classification systems of Europe, America and Asia. Descriptive naturalists were mystified by animals they could not classify at all. They were almost as amazed by the animals of Australia as the earliest explorers had been, but the discovery of a platypus in 1797 caused more perplexity than anything previously discovered. This 'amphibious animal of the mole species' which lived on the banks of freshwater lagoons in New South Wales was drawn by Governor Hunter before he sent a specimen to England. The naturalists who received a badly preserved specimen could only suspect a hoax.

One of the foremost naturalists of the day George Shaw, in describing the platypus in his long-running series the *Naturalists' Miscellany,* wrote,

Of all the Mammalia yet known it seems the most extra-ordinary in its conformation; exhibiting the perfect resemblance of the beak of a Duck engrafted on the head of a quadruped . . .

Rusty hood *Pterostylis rufa*, an Australian plant grown from seed at Kew. Drawn by Franz Bauer, official artist at Kew and brother of Ferdinand.
BM(NH)

Admitting freely that he doubted the testimony of his own eyes, even after the most minute and rigid examination, he could only conclude that 'on a subject so extraordinary as the present, a degree of scepticism is not only pardonable but laudable'. Suspecting that someone had assembled this animal from pieces, naturalists forbore to name it more clearly than as the 'paradox'. In 1803 Banks, who too had reservations, sent to George Caley in New South Wales for more information. 'Our greatest want here' he wrote, 'is to be acquainted with the manner in which the Duck Bill Animal and the Porcupine Ant Eater, which I think is of the same genus breed.' Their internal structure suggested rightly to Banks that the platypus might lay eggs. This puzzle was not sorted out until 1884.

Debate in all areas of science followed the consideration of specimens from Australia as classification systems had to be revised and conclusions abandoned. The most disturbing arguments went on for decades, however, over the animal kingdom. Beginning in the 1820s and 1830s, natural scientists were drawn into conflict with the established church over the evidence provided for theories of evolution.

Innocent of these pre-occupations, the British public was content to turn its attention and imagination to the amazing curiosities from Australia. Museums, botanical gardens and zoological parks were all features of an age in pursuit of enlightenment. There were many private museums, of varying quality, which provided displays for the general public.

Two of the most famous had originated with private collectors in the Midlands. The Leverian Museum of Alkrington Hall, Manchester, was owned by Sir Ashton Lever (1728–88) who had been given many prize specimens from Captain Cook's voyages by Joseph Banks, and who also acquired some specimens sent to England by surgeon John White.

Lever moved his museum to London in 1774 but found that despite a high admission charge the cost of maintaining and housing his ever-expanding collection too great. He offered it unsuccessfully to the British Museum then organized a lottery in 1797. The 1 guinea lottery was won by James Parkinson (the discoverer of Parkinson's Disease) who ran the museum for many years at Blackfriars, until he found himself facing the same problem as

Ashton Lever's Museum at Leicester House, London.

Lever. In 1806 he auctioned off the collection, taking over 2 months to dispose of all the items.

Bullock's Pantherion being displayed in the Egyptian Hall, London, helped to fill the gap, before its history followed the same course. A Sheffield jeweller, William Bullock, made a huge collection of some 32 000 rare items that he put on display in London. Bullock exhibited Australian plants and animals, such as the platypus, kangaroo, echidna, opossum, black swan and emu. He also added specimens from the Levenian Museum to his display. In 1790 a *Companion to the Museum* was issued according to its preface at the urging of 'many Persons of the most distinguished Learning and Abilities, Admirers of the Works of Nature in its almost infinite Variety of Forms and Properties . . .' but in 1815 Bullock, too, auctioned off the entire museum.

There were other ways in which specialist groups of people became aware of what was happening in New South Wales. Governor Phillip had sent a sample of clay from the settlement in 1788 which was given to Josiah Wedgwood for analysis. Wedgwood found it fit for the production of porcelain and made several medallions of it. This is one of the first successful efforts in the drive to find and analyse Australian natural products.

Interior of Bullock's Museum.

Colonial governors and Joseph Banks encouraged the search for minerals, and coal and iron ore samples were sent back to England. Cultivation of commercial crops of vines, cotton, tobacco, hemp and indigo was tried.

Banks was again to be instrumental in the breath-taking plans to develop an Australian wool industry. To escape the damaging dependence on the Spanish monopoly of fine wool during the Napoleonic War, some Merino sheep were smuggled out of Spain and used to establish a royal flock at Kew. It was intended to encourage farmers to rear fine-woolled sheep in place of traditional coarse-woolled breeds and thus support the major British cloth industry. Some early samples of wool from New South Wales caused Banks to arrange for Merinos from the King's flock to be sent there, and residents such as John Macarthur and the Revd Samuel Marsden, among others, were

encouraged with land grants and advice to advance the breeding of fine wool in the colony. Australian conditions were better than British ones for the Merinos. The first shipments were small and experimental.

Encouragement was constantly offered by the Royal Society of Arts throughout the decade for the development of export resources. In 1820 the Society offered two gold medals for the greatest quantity of fine wool imported from New South Wales. In 1822 John Macarthur won both medals with his consignment of 15 000 lbs of wool from the Merino strain that was being assiduously bred by a number of leading colonists. Further publicity followed when the Society awarded a silver medal to the Huddersfield manufacturers Starkey, Buckley & Co for the cloth they produced for the Society from Macarthur's wool. Other medals for wool and cloth were awarded until the trade in wool was firmly established.

The establishment of the wool industry was to have a profound effect on the development of Australia. It brought a demand for grazing land to pasture flocks. In 1813 the Blue Mountains were reached, and subsequently passed 2 years later to reveal a 'beautiful and Champain Country'. Earl Bathurst, the Colonial Secretary, responded enthusiastically, and described this as 'An Event in the History of New So (sic) Wales not more important on Account of its immediate Consequences than for the Effect, which it must ultimately produce in the Nature of Value of the Colony.' With the end of the Napoleonic war in 1815 British curiosity about Australia surrendered its scientific emphasis to a commercial concern, influenced by a sharp interest in the imperial economy. The appointment of Commissioner John Bigge, who reported on the state of the colony in 1821 and 1822, was one manifestation of this interest.

The character of New South Wales changed dramatically between 1820 and 1830. Commissioner Bigge recommended wool-growing for New South Wales and government was eager to encourage free settlers with capital by giving them generous grants of land on which to run flocks of wool-bearing sheep. The pressure mounted for grazing land as the flow of free settlers increased. Stockmen 'looking for grass and not for glory' moved into the interior.

In 1817 the British government decided that the remaining part of the Australian coastline which had not been surveyed by Flinders should be charted. Command of the maritime expedition was given to Lieutenant Phillip Parker King. the naval son of ex-governor King, who had been trained by the Admiralty hydrographer. He was instructed by the Admiralty to search for a waterway into the interior, and to examine the climate, biology and topography of the shore lines. Access to the interior was a paramount consideration and 'indeed, all gulfs and openings should be the objects of particular attention, as the chief motive for your survey is to discover whether there be any river on that part of the coast likely to lead to an interior navigation into this great continent'. King

Clay medallion fashioned by Josiah Wedgwood from clay sent from Sydney Cove.
WM

was accompanied on his several voyages by botanist Allan Cunningham (1791–1839) perhaps the most widely travelled scientific explorer in the history of Australian exploration.

Cunningham was the last of Banks's protégés. He arrived in Sydney in 1816 as King's botanist collecting for Kew Gardens under Banks's instructions and on his first expedition returned to Sydney with 'upwards of Five Hundred Plants totally different from those hitherto Collected or Known in this Country'. In 1823 Cunningham began a series of important explorations. 'I find that I can blend discovery with botanical research tolerably well,' he wrote. He found practical inland routes to the rich Liverpool Plains, Darling Downs, and to what is now southern Queensland, classifying some of his plants on the way into 'Grasses and Herbage valuable to the Farmer'. In 1828 he explored the Brisbane River to its source and returned to Sydney with 70 boxes of specimens of Queensland plants for Kew. Anxious to prevent loss of control, the government in 1829 proclaimed the boundary of settlement by defining the so-called 'nineteen counties'. But the momentum set up by would-be pastoralists and the pressures of a rapidly growing population could not be stemmed.

The main centres for the spread of settlement around the continent were nearly all defined within this decade. In 1824 convicts were shipped to Moreton Bay to set up a base that eventually became Brisbane. In 1826, prompted by the presence of the French expedition under D'Urville, a settlement was established at Westernport that soon failed. At Port Essington another short-lived settlement aimed to safeguard the north. In the west the Swan River colony (Perth) was founded in 1829. The last major centres to be established were Adelaide in 1836 and Port Phillip (Melbourne). The Port Phillip Association purchased 600 000 acres directly from the local natives for blankets, knives and trinkets in 1835. By June 1836 the foundation of the settlement of Melbourne had begun with an influx of 200 pioneers and 30 000 sheep – trespassers though they still were in the eyes of government.

The development that had been almost stationary during the 25 years of the Napoleonic war gathered momentum rapidly. By the mid 1820s there was a population of 30 000 in New South Wales and a picture of optimistic activity and the expectation of prosperity were clearly emerging. A member of one of the many French expeditions that visited Sydney between 1818 and 1826 wrote rapturously in 1819 of the 'Magnificent hotels, majestic mansions, houses of extraordinary taste and elegance, fountains ornamented with sculptures worthy of the chisels of our best artists . . .'

Though this assessment was perhaps over-indulgent there were sufficient signs of wealth to impress visitors. Commissioner Bigge had found 21 merchants in business in Sydney and 12 mercantile houses, three of them controlled by emancipists or ex-convicts. On Van Diemen's Land he listed 13 merchants. Even governors like Lachlan Macquarie, who administered New South Wales in 1810–21, and who was used to the careless magnificence of Bengal, was impressed by the stores, wharfs and elegant houses of his domain. Even the grudging eye of envy admitted that Sydney had its privileged who 'live in great houses, keep large retines, support extensive establishments and roll along in their splendid equipages'.

Alan Cunningham
(1790–1839)
botanical explorer.
By J E H Robinson,
watercolour.
LS

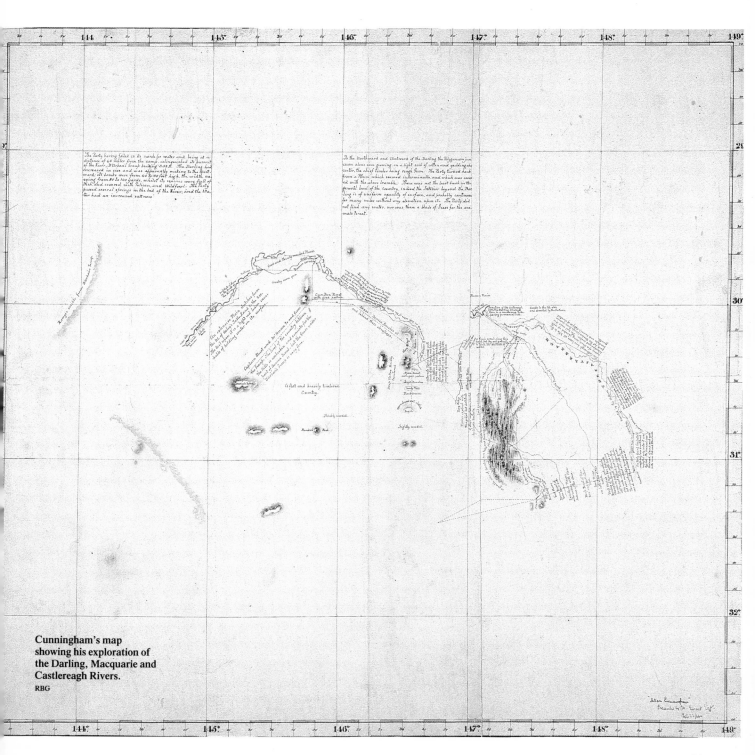

Cunningham's map
showing his exploration of
the Darling, Macquarie and
Castlereagh Rivers.
RBG

91

Sponsors

The Trustees and Director of the British Museum (Natural History) would like to thank the following for their support of the exhibition **First Impressions: The British Discovery of Australia** on which this publication is based:

THE AUSTRALIAN BICENTENNIAL AUTHORITY which was established by the Commonwealth Government of Australia to co-ordinate the celebrations in 1988 to mark the 200th anniversary of European settlement of Australia.

THE BRITAIN-AUSTRALIA BICENTENNIAL TRUST, the charitable arm of the Britain-Australia Bicentennial Committee which was established by Her Majesty's Government to encourage and co-ordinate a wide ranging programme of events and projects to ensure that Britain participates fully in the celebrations to mark the Australian Bicentenary.

THE BRITISH COUNCIL, which has supported the exhibition in both Britain and Australia. The aim of the Council is to promote an enduring understanding of Britain through cultural and educational co-operation.

CITIBANK LIMITED, the Australian subsidiary of Citibank NA, which is the sole sponsor of the exhibition in Australia. Citibank offers a spectrum of retail, corporate and investment banking services. It is part of a global organization which operates from 2991 offices in 93 countries on five continents.

THE COOKSON GROUP, a rapidly expanding British company with worldwide operations, produces specialized materials for industry. At the turn of the century, it was importing lead ingot from Broken Hill in Australia, and now it is one of the largest purchasers of mineral sands. These are converted into zirconium silicate, used as an opacifier for ceramic products, and into titanium dioxide, a major constituent in paint and paper manufacture. End products from Cookson materials are found in homes throughout the world.

THE CORPORATION OF LONDON, who generously supported the exhibition and other events in the Bicentennial Celebrations.

THE INTERNATIONAL CULTURAL CORPORATION OF AUSTRALIA, a public company created in 1980 by the Commonwealth Government of Australia for the management of major touring exhibitions.

'The International Cultural Corporation of Australia with the Australian Bicentennial Authority is delighted to contribute financially to the London season of **First Impressions**. We offer our congratulations to the British Museum (Natural History) for creating such a unique and lively exhibition in celebration of Australia's bicentenary, and look forward to touring the exhibition to seven Australian cities in 1988 and 1989.'
James B Leslie AO MC
Chairman ICCA

PRIVATE PATIENTS PLAN, a provident association whose main activity is the organization of private medical insurance. It is the second largest medical insurance company in the United Kingdom.

Bibliography

1966. *Australian Dictionary of Biography. Vol. 1, 1788–1850.* Melbourne University Press, Melbourne.

BEAGLEHOLE, J.C. (ed.).
The Journals of Captain Cook on his voyages of Discovery. Vol. 1 1955. *The Voyage of the Endeavour 1768–1771.* Cambridge University Press, Cambridge.

———1962.
The Endeavour Journal of Joseph Banks 1768–1771. 2 vols, Angus and Robertson, Sydney.

———1974.
The Life of Captain James Cook. Black, London.

BROCKWAY, L. 1979.
Science and Colonial Expansion: The Role of the British Royal Botanic Gardens. Academic Press, London and New York.

CARR, D.J. (ed.) 1983.
Sydney Parkinson, Artist of Cook's Endeavour Voyage. British Museum (Natural History)/Croom Helm, London and Canberra.

CARTER, H.B. 1964.
His Majesty's Spanish Flock. Sir Joseph Banks and the Merinos of George III of England. Angus and Robertson, Sydney.

———1987.
Sir Joseph Banks 1743–1820. British Museum (Natural History), London.

CURREY, J.E.B. 1966.
George Caley: Reflections on the Colony of New South Wales. Angus and Robertson, Melbourne.

FINNEY, C.M. 1984.
To Sail Beyond the Sunset. Natural History in Australia 1699–1829. Rigby, Adelaide.

GRANT, J. 1803.
The narrative of a Voyage of discovery performed in HMS Lady Nelson . . . to New South Wales. Nicol, London.

INGLETON, G. 1986.
Matthew Flinders. 2 vols, Genesis/Hedley, Surrey.

McMINN, W.G. 1970.
Allan Cunningham, Botanist and Explorer. Melbourne University Press, Melbourne.

PARKINSON, S. 1773.
Journal of a Voyage to the South Seas . . . Parkinson, London.

PERRY, T.M. 1982.
The Discovery of Australia. The Charts and Maps of the Navigators and Explorers. Hamish Hamilton, London and Melbourne.

PERRY. T.M. & SIMPSON, D.H. (eds). 1962.
William Westall, Drawings. Nelson, London.

RIENITS, R. & RIENITS, Y. 1963.
Early Artists of Australia. Sydney.

SMITH, B. 1985.
European Vision and the South Pacific 1768–1850. 2nd edition, Yale University Press, London and New Haven.

———1985.
The Art of Captain Cook's Voyages. 2 vols, Oxford University Press, Melbourne.

SPATE, O.H.K. 1983.
Spanish Lake – Pacific since Magellan. Vol. 2, *Monopolists and Freebooters.* Croom Helm, Canberra.

STEARN, W.T. (ed.) 1976.
The Australian Flower Paintings of Ferdinand Bauer. Basilisk Press, London.

WILSON, E.J. 1961.
James Lee and the Vineyard Nursery, Hammersmith. Arrowsmith, London.

Acknowledgements

Produced by the Department of Public Services,
British Museum (Natural History).
Designed by James Crew,
edited by Gail McKenzie,
photographic research by Robert Bloomfield,
photography by David Morbey.

We would like to thank the following
organizations for permission to reproduce
photographs in this book:

BL	British Library, London
BM	British Museum, London
BM(NH)	British Museum (Natural History)
FDC	Fielding Druce Herbarium, Oxford
LS	The Linnean Society of London
NMM	National Maritime Museum, London
NPG	National Portrait Gallery, London
RAL	Royal Architectural Library, London
RBG	Royal Botanic Gardens, Kew, London
RNK	Rex Nan Kivell Collection, National Library of Australia, Canberra
SM	Science Museum, London
WM	The Wedgwood Museum, Barlaston, England

Index